Raising Seed Money for Your Own Business

Raising Seed Money for Your Own Business

Brian R. Smith

The Lewis Publishing Company
Lexington, Massachusetts
Brattleboro, Vermont

To Vanessa Concordia Smith
Star Child

First Edition

Text copyright © 1984 by Brian R. Smith

This book is manufactured in the United States of America. It is designed by Irving Perkins Associates and published by The Lewis Publishing Company, Fessenden Road, Brattleboro, Vermont 05301.

Distributed in the United States by E. P. Dutton, Inc., New York.

Library of Congress Cataloging in Publication Data

Smith, Brian R., 1939–
   Raising seed money for your own business.

   Includes index.
   1. New business enterprises—Finance—Handbooks, manuals, etc. 2. Small business—Finance—Handbooks, manuals, etc. I. Title.
HG4027.6S64   1984   658.1′522   84–791
ISBN 0–86616–041–8

Contents

Acknowledgments

I would first like to thank Tom Begner, the president of the Lewis Publishing Company, for coming up with the basic idea for *Seed Money*. I am also grateful to the other fine folk there—Bob Enos, Kathy Shulga, Susan Kryger—who have helped along the way.

I want to thank three fine, professional bankers for their outstanding help on the chapter on commercial banks; Richard Dugger, the president of Ashuelot National Bank in Keene, New Hampshire, J. Reeve Cantus, Ashuelot's Executive Vice President, and John D. ("Rick") Hashagen, Jr., senior vice president of Vermont National Bank.

Ray Denault, the assistant director of management assistance for the U.S. Small Business Administration in Montpelier, Vermont, gave me much management assistance on the SBA chapter. Susan M. Kelsay of The Robert Morris Associates in Philadelphia was most helpful with new RMA data, and James S. Howard, the founder of Country Business Services, Inc., gave me valuable information for some of the self-assessment material in chapter two. Three former students of mine at Southern Vermont College—Debra Horton, Don Pasha, and Brad Silver—let me use parts of their student projects in this book.

Marjorie A. Zerbel of Jaffrey, New Hampshire, typed the entire manuscript for the book and was always able to meet production schedules. For that I am grateful beyond words.

Finally I want to thank the Dog Lady—Myrna M. Milani, DVM—for the painstaking editing job that she did on *Seed Money* before it went to typing.

IMPORTANT!!!
READ THE FOLLOWING!!!
HEREOF FAIL NOT AT YOUR PERIL!!!

SO YOU WANT TO START A BUSINESS? WELL, I'M ASSUMING YOU ARE OR YOU WOULDN'T HAVE PLUNKED DOWN THE PRICE FOR THIS BOOK. THIS BOOK HAS ONE PURPOSE—TO HELP GET YOU WHAT IS CALLED "SEED MONEY." MOST SMALL BUSINESSES GET THEIR SEED MONEY FROM THE PERSON WHO STARTS THE BUSINESS (THE ENTREPRENEUR, THE FOUNDER), SOME FRIENDS AND RELATIVES OF THE ENTREPRENEUR, AND A COMMERCIAL BANK. BUT MOST PEOPLE GO ABOUT IT ALL WRONG. THEY GO TO THE SOURCES OF MONEY TOO SOON. THIS BOOK WILL SHOW YOU THE RIGHT WAY TO GO ABOUT IT. NOT BRAG, FACT! I'M NOT GOING TO START OUT TALKING ABOUT MONEY. I'M GOING TO START TALKING ABOUT BUSINESS AND SOME PRELIMINARY THINKING YOU MUST DO. AFTER CHAPTER ONE, YOU'LL NEED A PEN OR A PENCIL BECAUSE WE'RE GOING TO BE WORKING TOGETHER AS WE GO ALONG. YOU CAN'T GO TO THE BANK WITHOUT A BUSINESS PLAN, AND I'LL SHOW YOU HOW TO DO ONE—STEP-BY-STEP. NO SWEAT. OTHERS HAVE DONE IT. AFTER YOU DO YOUR PLAN, THEN I'LL TELL YOU HOW TO APPROACH FRIENDS, RELATIVES, BANKS, AND PRIVATE INVESTORS. YOU CAN'T GO TO THEM UNTIL YOU DO YOUR HOMEWORK—HOMEWORK GOOD ENOUGH FOR AN "A" BY MY STANDARDS, AND I'M TOUGH! I MAY PICK ON YOU A BIT JUST TO MAKE SURE THAT YOU ARE, IN FACT, AN ENTREPRENEUR, NOT AN ARMCHAIR OBSERVER OR A DREAMER. I'LL MAKE YOU QUESTION YOURSELF AND YOUR MOTIVES FOR WANTING TO TAKE THIS ROAD, BUT I'LL DO IT BEFORE SOME BANKER OR RICH UNCLE DOES, EMBARRASSES YOU, AND THEN SENDS YOU PACKING. I'LL TELL YOU HOW TO GET YOUR SEED MONEY, BUT YOU MUST FOLLOW ALONG WITH THE WAY I PUT THIS BOOK TOGETHER. NO SKIPPING AROUND. NO SHORTCUTS. NONE OF THIS STUFF ABOUT, "I KNOW IT ALL ANYWAY." YOU DON'T.

IF YOU DO WHAT I SAY, YOU'LL GET YOUR MONEY. THERE'S

ONE EXCEPTION, THOUGH. IF SOMEWHERE DEEP DOWN YOU REALLY DON'T WANT TO BE IN BUSINESS AND/OR YOU'RE DOING THIS WHOLE THING BECAUSE YOU'RE ON SOME KIND OF EGO TRIP—"HEY, MAN, THERE GOES DICK. HE OWNS HIS OWN BUSINESS. MAN, IS HE IMPORTANT."—OR IF YOU THINK YOU'VE HIT ON SOME GET-RICH-QUICK SCHEME, THEN YOU PROBABLY WON'T MAKE IT, REGARDLESS OF WHAT I TELL YOU.

NOW, WHAT I SUGGEST IS YOU SLOWLY SKIM THE ENTIRE BOOK FIRST TO GET A BASIC IDEA OF WHAT I'M CONVEYING. THEN START READING AND DOING—CAREFULLY AND HONESTLY.

BRIAN R. SMITH
Entrepreneur

October 1983

Overview and Organization

CHAPTER One

The purpose of this book is simple. It is a guide and a workbook to enable individual men and women, regardless of their age, ethnic background, business experience, education, or state of personal finances, to start a business of their own and to get their seed money. Personal characteristics or traits have little to do with beginning a successful small business. I have personally seen instances where people with MBAs and 20 years of sophisticated business experience fail in getting a startup off the ground because they were a bit smug about what they believed made a business successful. Sometimes having "all the money in the world" leads to sloppy practices which eventually spell disaster. What makes a small business successful? The desire on the part of the entrepreneur to succeed. It's that simple.

The book is a guide to get you going and keep you on track. The methodology, although clear and logical, will not guarantee success. You must do that. However, by following this material, you'll greatly lessen the probability of failure.

This book is intended for individuals who plan to start a business rather than buy an operating one. Purchasing a going concern is a much more complex procedure and normally requires more professional help; so if you also have an interest in buying a business, I suggest you contact a business broker.

The methods and approaches in this book will work regardless of the type of business you're considering. What kind of business appeals to you? Most businesses in the United States are classified in one of six broad categories:

1. *Retail.* A retail business—a small grocery store, a clothing shop, a mail order operation, or a home sales business—sells goods directly to individual consumers or groups. The number of goods sold to any one customer is generally small.
2. *Wholesale.* Wholesalers (older term: "middlemen") like beer distributors must often purchase goods directly from a manufacturer or processor and then re-sell those goods to another type of business, most often a retail business. The purchase and resale of these goods are normally in large quantities.
3. *Service.* Enterprises that don't supply tangible goods are service businesses. They include hair salons, lawn care establishments, shoe repair shops, professional services (law, medical, accounting).

1

4. *Manufacturing.* Anyone who makes something is called a manufacturer whether it's a massive computer or a wooden knick-knack. Manufacturers are often called "converters" because they take raw material and change or convert it.

5. *Transportation.* Transportation companies move things from one place to another, usually freight and/or people. Normally transportation businesses are categorized as trucking (contract, common carrier, and packages like UPS), air, water, and pipeline.

6. *Construction.* A construction business builds things. If it builds houses and buildings, it is called vertical construction, whereas flat things like roads and airfields are built by firms in horizontal construction.

Of course, there are combinations of business types, such as an artisan engaged in making pottery (manufacturing) and then selling his or her wares to the general public (retail). There are also special categories such as mining, fishing, and lumbering.

Also, although this book is not specifically for non-profit organizations, much of the general approach will work. If you are considering operating a not-for-profit business, such as a children's day care center, you should consult your local Internal Revenue Service office for their latest regulations regarding what is commonly called a "501(c)3," a non-profit business. You will also need legal and accounting help from specialists who have experience forming non-profits.

Using This Book

This book contains exercises and forms that are meant to be used as you go along. Some of the forms can be removed and used with financing sources like banks or private investors. Other exercises are strictly for your own analysis. I'll explain how to use the forms as we go along and will, from time to time, have other suggestions for you. When I offer a particular suggestion, such as using an attorney, I do it for one very strong reason: I believe that it's necessary for your business success.

Small Business Failure

More startups fail than succeed. That's a fact of life. Although actual statistics are impossible to come by, the figure quoted most often is that for every ten businesses started, eight of these ventures will not last five years. To be sure, that figure is "loaded" because some businesses are not started with the intent of keeping them running forever. Others are sold or merge into another business and thereby lose their identity; but a conservative estimate puts the odds against you rather than in your favor. Purchasing a going concern approximately doubles your chances of success, but even that route contains risk. Thus it is extremely important that you ground yourself in some basic material before you rush headlong into an area in which many people learn their lessons too late.

Dun & Bradstreet (D&B) collects annual statistics on business failure and categorizes those failures according to reason for failure, type of business, age of business, and geography. Most of these statistics relate to larger businesses, but the overall patterns are applicable to all. An interesting fact is that the reasons for failure are approximately the same from one year to the next.

The underlying causes of most business failures in the United States can be traced to inexperience and incompetence on the part of management. Of the 11,742 businesses that D&B tracked in 1980, 95 percent of the failures were traced to:

1. lack of experience in the particular line of the business;
2. lack of managerial experience;
3. unbalanced experience (not well-rounded enough in marketing, finance, purchasing);
4. incompetence.

The *business* reasons for failure can be traced primarily to an inability on the part of the business owner(s) or manager(s) to avoid conditions that result in inadequate sales, heavy operating expenses, competitive weaknesses (i.e., being undone by competitors), and difficulty in collecting or financing receivables (money owed to the business by customers).

Contrary to popular opinion, less than 2 percent of the businesses that fail do so because of disaster, neglect, or fraud. In other words, most businesses fail as a result of inside mistakes, not external factors. Calling a spade a spade, businesses fail because those operating them do dumb things. Period.

How long do poorly run businesses last? The greater number, almost one-third, fail in either the third or fourth year of operation. Less than 1 percent fail in their first year, probably because the owner has enough capital to keep even a very bad idea going for a year or two.

And finally, many entrepreneurs fail because they want to. That statement may seem totally ludicrous, but I've run into many people who feel they're not worthy or deserving of success. In essence, these folks build failure into their businesses from the very start and then get what they want. Confidence in starting and running a business means that you don't fear risk—you reduce any fear by acquiring information and using it to operate a successful venture. The business can only be successful if the entrepreneur sees himself or herself as a personal success. That must be accomplished before you go into business; you can't expect to have a business *make* you a success. Wealthy maybe. But not successful. Money is a thing. Success is a feeling. They aren't equated unless you set it up that way.

Starting vs. Buying a Business

Starting a business is the height of entrepreneurship. If we construct a continuum based on an arbitrary system of one to ten, ten representing a maximum entrepreneurial rating, we may categorize the entire spectrum as shown in Figure 1-1.

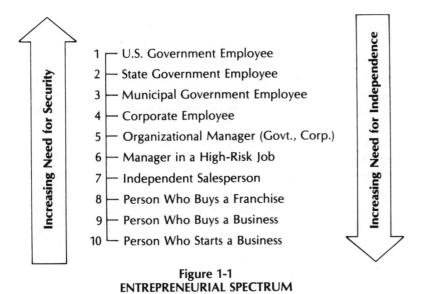

1	U.S. Government Employee
2	State Government Employee
3	Municipal Government Employee
4	Corporate Employee
5	Organizational Manager (Govt., Corp.)
6	Manager in a High-Risk Job
7	Independent Salesperson
8	Person Who Buys a Franchise
9	Person Who Buys a Business
10	Person Who Starts a Business

Increasing Need for Security

Increasing Need for Independence

Figure 1-1
ENTREPRENEURIAL SPECTRUM

The spectrum demonstrates the balance between two variables—the need for security and the need for independence. It doesn't show that entrepreneurs are better than government employees; it simply indicates that their needs are different. Government employees are "RIF'd"* with probably the same frequency that small business owners fail. The point is that starting a business takes a different kind of person than buying a business or a franchise.

When you buy a business, many elements of that business are already in place. There is an existing product or service; the business has a name and a location; it may have employees; it certainly has customers. When you start a business, you begin with only an idea and yourself. Unlike buying a going concern, starting a business means you must:

1. choose the legal form—proprietorship, partnership, corporation;
2. pick a name;
3. decide upon the product or service;
4. provide startup capital;
5. select the customer group that you want to sell to;
6. start the venture into motion and overcome the great inertia that exists for anything new.

One very interesting fact, and one few people are aware of, is that it takes more money to start a business than it does to buy an established one. The major reason for this is that the purchase of a going concern includes a host of "free" things. Some of these things are tangible: a business telephone, established files, employee policies. Others, such as reputation, are intangible. Let's use the business telephone as an example: a new business owner will spend time with the phone company, there will be a delay from time of request to time of installation, a security deposit will be required, and possibly the first month's estimated charges will have to be paid in advance. When you buy an established business, all this has already been done.

The major advantage of a startup is that there's no need to do everything at once. Some people who start their own businesses may spend years getting it going, working at it part-time (evenings, weekends) while maintaining a full-time job. Then, when the economic conditions are appropriate, they switch over to full-time operation. We'll discuss the issue of timing in relation to full-time business operation in detail later.

Before We Begin

We're about to begin a journey into entrepreneurship. Before we do, there are a few thoughts I'd like you to consider. This book is intended to help get you going financially, but that's not the major concern of a business. The primary emphasis of a business must be marketing; if a business owner fails to perform careful marketing research and then supply the needed products or services to the proper customer group, all the money in the Chase Manhattan Bank or the Morgan Guaranty Trust will not bring about business success.

When many professionals—bank officers, accountants, attorneys—evaluate a business that failed, they invariably say the reason for the failure was a lack of capital. Essentially they're correct as far as they go, but saying a business dies from insufficient cash is like a physician saying that a person dies from lack of blood after a major artery is ruptured in an automobile accident. Almost every business failure I see can be traced to basic errors in marketing—pricing too high or low, wrong market, inattention to customer needs, failure

---

* A term that comes from the U.S. military meaning "Reduction In Force."

to notice what competition is doing, difficulty in collecting receivables. If you feel, after going through the explanations and exercises in this book, that you need more background in marketing, I suggest one or more of the following:

1. Contact an individual consultant with marketing expertise.
2. Attend a seminar on marketing.
3. Enroll in a marketing course at a local college.
4. Read marketing books such as my *Successful Marketing for Small Business* (1984, The Lewis Publishing Co., Brattleboro, VT 05301).

Getting a business off the ground financially is somewhat like starting your car. When you turn the ignition key, electrical power is borrowed from the battery and applied to the starter motor and spark plugs. If the engine is unable to start on its own because of some internal problem, power drains from the battery until there is insufficient electrical energy to start the motor. If, on the other hand, all is working well, the engine fires and runs on its own, putting borrowed power back into the battery via the alternator.

If your business is to operate successfully, you will use your own money and probably funds from some outside source (bank, friends, private investors) only to start the business. At some point it, too, must "fire" on its own and then repay those borrowed funds. If there's a fatal flaw in the business (and it's usually a marketing one), the business draws off the initial funds until they are depleted.

Dun & Bradstreet, in a booklet entitled "The Pitfalls in Managing a Small Business," lists the key problem areas for business owners:

1. Lack of experience.
2. Lack of money.
3. The wrong location.
4. Improper inventory management.
5. Too much capital in fixed assets.
6. Poor credit practices.
7. Taking too much for yourself.
8. Unplanned expansion.
9. Having the wrong attitude.

Fully two-thirds of the above items—numbers 2, 3, 4, 5, 7, and 8—can be eliminated by completing a business plan before you start the actual business. (We'll spend all of Chapter Four on business plans). The first item, lack of experience, has an interesting Catch-22 to it: you'll never have the experience you need to start your first business because you've never done it before. It's sort of like electing a new U.S. president. The thing to remember is that *millions* of people have started successful businesses before you, some with less experience than you. You can gain experience by proxy, though. Talk to others who have started their own ventures; interview professionals such as accountants and attorneys to help entrepreneurs get started; plan a visit with a bank commercial loan officer; go to your nearest SBA office (see Appendix A) and talk to the management assistance officers as well as SCORE (Service Corps of Retired Executives) and ACE (Active Corps of Executives), people who work with the SBA and help entrepreneurs. You may even want to work in someone else's new business for a while.

Item number 6, poor credit practices, is the major factor that sank W. T. Grant. They mailed out hundreds of thousands of their own credit cards with little attention to whom they were sending this plastic money. My advice is to be extremely careful when extending credit. (For a full discussion of credit and collection, see the marketing book referenced earlier and also credit literature from the SBA.) If you're going to start a retail business or a service business, become a VISA and/or Master Card merchant, which will essentially take you out of the business of having to provide your own credit. Your bank can assist you in this process.

The last item on Dun & Bradstreet's list, having the wrong attitude, is a unique issue. It's immeasurable, although it's possible to detect it. In the next chapter we'll discuss the concepts of entrepreneurship and I'll have some exercises for you to complete, but here are some common wrong attitudes I've come across in my travels:

1. Ego trips. Using a business to give some kind of status or false prestige.
2. Revenge. Starting a business just to get back at someone, usually a former employer. I've even seen a case or two in which an ex-spouse was the target.
3. Last ditch stand. Once in a while I find a person getting into business because he or she can't seem to find a job. They really are people who should be employed rather than self-employed.
4. Fantasy. Living where I do in northern New England, I see this one on a fairly regular basis. Some starry-eyed person or couple wanders up to Vermont from Manhattan looking for something that isn't there—like a large enough customer base to support some business idea that they have. A fantasy, in the larger sense, can be any business idea that won't fly because of the lack of a sufficient market.
5. Greed. Combine this one with the first item, ego trips, and you have an absolutely unbeatable formula for failure. No doubt about it. Get your kicks from your independence, not your savings account balance. It's possible to become financially well-off in your own business, but don't make that your primary goal. Serve others first.

Now we're ready to begin the next chapter, "Are You An Entrepreneur?" Find yourself a pen or a pencil because you're going to need it.

Are You An Entrepreneur?

CHAPTER TWO

Although definitions of the word entrepreneur vary widely, the one I like is "someone who starts a business and runs it successfully." There are varying degrees of entrepreneurial activity as I suggested in Figure 1-1 and it might be a good idea to review that spectrum now. In this chapter, there will be some exercises for you to complete; if you feel you need even more, I recommend: *New Venture Creation,* by Jeffry A. Timmons, Leonard E. Smollen, and Alexander L. M. Dingee, Jr. (1977, Richard D. Irwin, Inc., Homewood, IL 60430). Although the book is intended more for high-technology startups, there are many thought-provoking and interesting exercises in it. You might also consider an intensive (and expensive) two-weekend course called "The School for Entrepreneurs." For information, write to:

Registrar, The Tarrytown Group
Tarrytown House Executive Conference Center
East Sunnyside Lane
Tarrytown, NY 10591.

You're now ready to take a quiz. As in all exercises, it's most important that you answer the questions honestly and objectively.

Entrepreneurial Assessment

1. Are you willing to take moderate risks in life to achieve the goals you want? (Please notice the use of the word "moderate." Entrepreneurs are not crap shooters.)
   - ☐ Yes
   - ☐ No
   - ☐ Uncertain

2. Can you operate within an environment that is somewhat ill-defined and may even, from time to time, be chaotic?
   - ☐ Yes
   - ☐ No
   - ☐ Uncertain

3. Do you possess the drive and energy to work long hours to achieve what you want?
   - ☐ Yes
   - ☐ No
   - ☐ Uncertain

4. Are you prepared to place the needs of your business above those of your friends, your family, your community?
   - ☐ Yes
   - ☐ No
   - ☐ Uncertain

5. Are you the kind of person who can take full responsibility for both your successes and your failures?
   - ☐ Yes
   - ☐ No
   - ☐ Uncertain

7

6. Are your failures merely learning experiences for you?

☐ Yes
☐ No
☐ Uncertain

7. Do you need to be in control of your own working environment?

☐ Yes
☐ No
☐ Uncertain

8. Are you comfortable around strangers?

☐ Yes
☐ No
☐ Uncertain

9. Can you say "no" to someone you believe is trying to get you to do something that you don't want to do?

☐ Yes
☐ No
☐ Uncertain

10. When the need arises, can you tackle and complete a job that may not interest you?

☐ Yes
☐ No
☐ Uncertain

11. Are you willing to work hard to acquire new skills?

☐ Yes
☐ No
☐ Uncertain

12. Can you lead and inspire others?

☐ Yes
☐ No
☐ Uncertain

13. Can you take harsh criticism, even on a personal level?

☐ Yes
☐ No
☐ Uncertain

14. Are you able to hold onto your ideas and ideals even in the face of mass opinion that is counter to what you believe?

☐ Yes
☐ No
☐ Uncertain

For the next six statements, check the box that reflects your feelings.

15. It is more important to accomplish what I want than to earn a great deal of money.

☐ Agree
☐ Disagree
☐ Uncertain

16. People learn more from their mistakes than they do from their successes.

☐ Agree
☐ Disagree
☐ Uncertain

17. "Slow and steady wins the race."

☐ Agree
☐ Disagree
☐ Uncertain

18. It is not necessary to cut corners or compromise in order to succeed.

☐ Agree
☐ Disagree
☐ Uncertain

19. I value intangible qualities like love and wisdom over money and possessions.

☐ Agree
☐ Disagree
☐ Uncertain

20. There is no other person that I would rather be than me at this moment.

☐ Agree
☐ Disagree
☐ Uncertain

To score this self-assessment, give five points for every "Yes" or "Agree," three points for "Uncertain," and zero for "No" or "Disagree." Your total score will be between 0 and 100; you can then give yourself a letter grade:

90–100:	A
80–89:	B
70–79:	C
60–69:	D
below 60:	F

Before we go on to the rest of the assessments, I want to comment on two qualities of successful entrepreneurs that run counter to popular belief. One involves money and the other involves risk-taking. Much of the general public views entrepreneurs as individuals who take inordinately high risks and are only in business to make lots of money. Both views are wrong. Someone once asked me what entrepreneurs do at a roulette table. Do they play the single numbers which have a high risk-reward payoff or are they more likely to play odd-even or red-black, the "safest" combinations? My answer was that true entrepreneurs don't play at all because they know the odds of the house are against them. Regarding the issue of money, small business owners must understand economic values because ours is a free enterprise system; but it's far better to make the money issue a measurement of progress rather than an end in itself. Your heart is where your real treasure is. If you focus only on money, then you may fall victim to bottom-line performance at all costs, forgetting your own personal fulfillment and the commitment to serve others.

Business and Skills Assessment

Let's now move into some areas that will enable you to think about your desires and skills in the business area. The first of these checklists gives you an opportunity to set down some of the beginning criteria for your new business. If you're unclear about some of these items, leave those blank for now, but keep in mind that they should be settled in the future. The second list will enable you to assess the skills that are important in running a successful business. If you find there are large gaps in your business skills, you may need to gain more knowledge and experience.

BUSINESS CRITERIA

1. Where will this business be located (town, state)?

2. When will I begin the business (month, year)? [*Note:* Even if you are highly unsure of your timing, estimate this as closely as possible.]

3. My business must eventually have the following characteristics: [*Note:* These could be measurable quantities like sales of $500,000 or intangible items such as quality.]

   a.

   b.

   c.

   d.

   e.

4. My business must *not* have the following characteristics:

    a.

    b.

    c.

    d.

    e.

5. Here is a list of businesses (restaurant, office service firm, mail order) that are appealing to me:

    a.

    b.

    c.

    d.

    e.

6. Here is a list of businesses that do not appeal to me:

    a.

    b.

    c.

    d.

    e.

7. My lifestyle demands that I earn the following annual salary:

    $_____

8. I eventually want to work _____ hours per week:
    - ☐ less than 20
    - ☐ 20 to 40
    - ☐ 40 to 60
    - ☐ 60 to 80
    - ☐ more than 80

9. Which of the following best applies to me? (More than one could apply):
    - ☐ I want to keep the business small.
    - ☐ I want the business to grow to a moderate size.
    - ☐ I want to start a business that could grow quite large.
    - ☐ I will probably run the business for the rest of my life.
    - ☐ I will build the business, sell it, and start another.
    - ☐ I will build the business, sell it, and retire or do something else.
    - ☐ Other. Specify:

10. Who will be my primary customer(s)?
    - ☐ The consumer (the general public)
    - ☐ Other businesses or industry
    - ☐ Professional organizations (accountants, lawyers)

☐ Non-profit organizations (YMCAs, churches)
☐ Special groups (farmers, pilots)
     Specify:

☐ State or local government
☐ Federal government
☐ Foreign (export)
☐ Other. Specify:

11. What kind of a business will this be? (Review Chapter One if necessary).

  ☐ Retail
  ☐ Wholesale
  ☐ Service
  ☐ Transportation
  ☐ Construction
  ☐ Manufacturing
  ☐ Other. Specify:

12. Will there be others starting this business with you?

  ☐ No
  ☐ Yes

If yes, list person(s) and relationship (friend, spouse) if any:

	Name	**Relationship**
a.		
b.		
c.		

13. Who will be my advisors?

	Name	**Address**
a. Attorney		
b. Accountant		
c. Insurance Agent		
d. Consultant		
e. Other		

14. How will I sell my products or services?

  ☐ Me
  ☐ Employed salespeople
  ☐ Sales representatives (non-employees)
  ☐ Distributors/dealers
  ☐ Mail
  ☐ Other. Specify:

15. List below any assured income from trust, real estate investments, and the like:

	Source	Estimated Annual Income
a.		
b.		
c.		

16. Make a list below of any relatives or friends who might be approached for money later on:

	Name	Relationship
a.		
b.		
c.		
d.		
e.		

17. What are my important reasons for wanting to go into my own business? [*Note:* More than one may apply.]

☐ Believe I can "do it better" than existing competition.
☐ It's a dream. (No negative intent.)
☐ Don't like where I live now.
☐ Can't work for someone else.
☐ Want to make a lot of money.
☐ Want independence.
☐ Quit my job.
☐ Was fired.
☐ Fed up with corporate life.
☐ Want legacy for my children.
☐ Need tax shelter.
☐ Want to prove myself.
☐ Can't get along with bosses.
☐ Have unused talents.
☐ Want to do it my way without compromise.
☐ Want to be of real service to others.
☐ Family can work together.
☐ Other. Specify:

18. What are my major reservations about being in business?

☐ Fear of failure.
☐ Lack of business knowledge.
☐ Too much work.
☐ Giving up present pay and benefits.
☐ Leaving/losing present friends.
☐ No time for family.
☐ Giving up present outside activities.
☐ Might get locked in.
☐ Lack of confidence.
☐ Not enough money of my own.
☐ Not knowing where to turn for help.

☐ Acting impulsively.
☐ Acting too slowly.
☐ Fear of success.
☐ The entire question of risk.
☐ Fear of change.
☐ Discomfort with ill-defined situation—the unknown.
☐ Other. Specify:

19. What makes me think this business will succeed?

☐ Location
☐ Product or service.
☐ People on my team.
☐ Fills special market need.
☐ Others have done it.
☐ Have time to do it right.
☐ Low capital requirements.
☐ Other. Specify:

20. What are the weaknesses of this business as I see it now?

☐ Location.   ☐ Heavy capital requirements.
☐ Product or service.   ☐ Stiff competition.
☐ People on my team.   ☐ Idea too new or untried.
☐ Limited market.   ☐ Legal requirements.
                                 ☐ Other. Specify:

SKILLS CHECKLIST

I believe I have sufficient knowledge and background to run my own business.

Business Skill	Yes	No	Uncertain

I. SALES AND MARKETING

A. Marketing Research—Discovering market conditions and analyzing customer demand.

B. Marketing Planning—Using marketing research to construct strategy necessary to reach the market.

C. Pricing—Setting final prices that will be profitable but not out of reach of the customer.

D. Advertising/Public Relations —Using both message and media in a proper balance to increase customer demand and awareness.

E. Sales Management—Supervising others in the selling process.

*I believe I have sufficient knowledge and
background to run my own business.*

Business Skill	Yes	No	Uncertain

F. Personal Selling—Am I or can I be an effective salesperson?

G. Sales Administration—Knowledge of marketing law.

H. Competitive Analysis—Keeping abreast of what my competition is doing.

II. BUSINESS OPERATION

A. Purchasing—Knowing how to buy goods and services at minimum prices and best terms.

B. Inventory Control—Keeping supplies and raw materials at levels that are neither too high nor too low.

C. Scheduling—When to make certain events in a business occur for maximum effectiveness: a sense of timing.

D. Quality Control—How much effort to expend toward assuring proper quality consistent with price and customer expectation.

E. Business Planning—How to prepare and follow a business plan.

F. Expansion—Knowing how to plan for and use growth without running out of control.

III. FINANCE

A. Bookkeeping—The recording of accounting information in journals and ledgers.

B. Accounting — Understanding the key financial statements of a business, the income statement, and the balance sheet.

C. Budgeting—Doing a cash flow projection and using deviations to analyze estimated vs. actual performance.

D. Cost Control—Not only being able to detect excess expenses but doing something about it.

I believe I have sufficient knowledge and background to run my own business.

Business Skill	Yes	No	Uncertain

E. Credit & Collection—Knowing the proper circumstances in which to extend or deny credit and being able to collect overdue accounts.

F. Raising Money—Ability to deal with banks and other financial sources to secure capital.

G. Banking Relations—Knowing what banks expect from a small business.

H. Breakeven Analysis—How to do it; what it means.

I. Ratio Analysis—Using financial ratios to further assess information on the income statement and balance sheet.

J. Taxes—A basic understanding of the difference between personal and business taxes.

IV. ADMINISTRATION

A. Team Building—Selecting team members, hiring, firing, training, motivating, and leading.

B. Personnel Policies—Pay and benefits, labor guidelines, tax withholding, payroll reports (federal and state).

C. Dealing with Professionals—Accountants, attorneys, consultants, the SBA.

D. Using Information—Where to get information and how to put it to proper use.

E. Technology—The use of devices such as small business computers and word processors.

F. Business Law—A basic understanding of what is legal and illegal.

TOTALS _____ _____ _____

NOTE: There are 30 items in the skills checklist. You should have a *minimum* of 15 in the "YES" column.

Congratulations! You've just completed three crucial exercises about yourself and your business. If you've been honest, you should now have a fair idea of where you're headed, what you've got to help get you there, and what additional knowledge, skills, and information you may need. Again, no one ever has everything they need in a small business and in a way that's part of the fun. Being inquisitive as well as acquisitive is a part of the constant growing process; you'll never have to worry about burn-out as an entrepreneur.

Go back now and review what you've learned from the three exercises. In the first one, the Entrepreneurial Assessment, you gave yourself a letter grade. If that grade was a "D" or an "F," examine the categories in which you did not answer "yes" or "agree." Make a list of those personal items where you fall short and then ask yourself what barriers and beliefs stand in your way for making changes. The second exercise dealt with business criteria. If a large number of the questions were left blank, then you are probably some time away from starting your venture. Look carefully at the items that need to be resolved. Work on resolving them. Finally, you completed a skills checklist. There are four categories—sales and marketing, business operation, finance, administration. See if any of those categories have a majority of "no" and "uncertain" checks. If so, this should lead you to areas of study and learning. For example, if the finance section is particularly weak, you may want to take a standard two-semester course in accounting. Don't start your own business until you have satisfied *yourself* that you are ready, both personally and professionally.

If, as a potential business owner, you haven't decided to stop dead in your tracks, you're now ready to begin giving more serious thought to the actual business itself. We will begin that process in Chapter Three.

Initial Considerations

Now I want to make you aware of some thinking and planning that you must do before beginning a business operation. Many entrepreneurs learn these lessons through failure their first time. I know—I did.

In this chapter we'll cover:

1. The present state of your personal finances.
2. The legal form of your business.
3. Selecting your advisors.
4. Simple marketing research.
5. Timing.

Your Finances

In this section you're going to do two things: calculate your net worth and figure out what you need to live on. Both assessments are vitally important. Let's begin with what you're worth in dollars and cents, your net worth.

In a net worth statement you assign a monetary value to the things you own (assets), the things you owe (liabilities), and subtract the liabilities from the assets; the result is your net worth. If your liabilities are greater than your assets, your net worth will be negative and you will be in a *technical* state known as insolvency. You're not bankrupt—that's a *legal* state resulting from a ruling of a federal bankruptcy court.

A net worth statement, like the balance sheet of a business, shows what happens if you convert all your assets to cash and pay off all your liabilities. Ideally, you're left with a bunch of money. It's important to analyze this because if you're like most people who get into their own business, you're going to use some or most of your assets (cash in life insurance policies, a mutual fund, part of your pension, pledge your house as collateral for a business loan at a bank), to provide capital for your enterprise. It's doubtful you'll find all the necessary funding for your startup from outside sources. It does happen but it's extremely rare and, for reasons we'll discuss later, you might put yourself at a severe disadvantage by not providing a majority of the financing yourself. A final reason for doing a net worth analysis is that you'll need one when you apply for a bank loan. Bankers call a net worth statement a Statement of Financial Condition.

You can use the form on the next page to do your net worth statement. Note a net worth statement has a date on it; this is because it represents a snapshot of your financial condition at a specific moment in time, a frozen frame, if you will. If today is Tuesday, June 7, 1985, your finances will be different from next Tuesday, June 14th. In the intervening week, you may deposit a paycheck in your checking account, increasing your net worth; or, maybe the 100 shares of Engulf and Devour that you own drop five points, decreasing your net worth by $500. Note that assets are on the left and liabilities on the right. This is merely convention—there's no magic to this alignment.

Let's start with the asset (left) side. When recording amounts, don't worry about getting figures to the nearest penny. If you're within $50 of the exact figure, that's good enough.

Cash on hand: This means greens in your jeans or, as my grandfather used to say, cash money. Although most people don't carry a lot of money around with them, some folks keep cash hidden in piggy banks and the like. So, if you have some little mad money stashed away in a coffee can or a mattress, include it.

Cash in banks: Next to real cash money, funds in banks are the next best thing. Figure your actual checking account(s) balance for the day you

Net Worth Statement of _____

as of _____ **19__**

Assets		Liabilities	
Cash on hand	$	Notes payable to banks	$
Cash in banks		Secured	
Checking		Unsecured	
Savings		Amounts payable to others	
Other		Secured	
Money Market		Unsecured	
U. S. Govt. securities		Accounts due	
Marketable securities		Credit cards	
Stocks		Installment loans	
Bonds		Other	
Mutual Funds			
Other			
Receivables			
Life Insurance (CSV)		Unpaid taxes	
Real Estate		Insurance loans	
Vehicles		Mortgages	
Personal property		Other debts	
Pension benefits		TOTAL LIABILITIES	$
Business interests		NET WORTH	$
Other Assets			
TOTAL ASSETS	$	LIABILITIES AND NET WORTH	$

choose to do your net worth statement. If you haven't balanced your checking account, do it now. If you have a savings account, or several, call the bank and ask them to calculate any interest due. (In the category called "Other" you may have certificates of deposit, CDs. Again, it's important to include any accrued interest on CDs; your local banking officer or head teller can give you this information.)

Money Market: In the late 1970's when interest rates reached 20 percent, many people performed disintermediation, that is, switching funds from one source (bank savings accounts) to another, the new money market funds. If you still have one of these, write in the balance as well as any accrued interest.

U.S. Government Securities: There seem to be hundreds of kinds of government securities—treasury notes, treasury bonds, Series E bonds, Series H bonds, Fannie Maes, Ginnie Maes, repos, treasury bills, and on and on. If you have any of these, put down their present values.

Marketable Securities: For stocks—both common and preferred—give their market value on the date of the net worth statement. If you own stock in a company that's not publicly traded, you'll need to determine its value. If you own restricted stock, it's better not to assign any value to it at all because it's not "marketable." Bonds include such items as convertible debentures, corporate bonds, municipal bonds, and the like. For mutual funds, you need what's called the net asset value (NAV) which you can determine by checking the Wall Street Journal. (For the category called "Other" you should include any items such as options, [puts and calls], commodity contracts, foreign bonds, margin accounts; remember, though, they must be *marketable.*)

Receivables: If any person or business owes you money, it's a receivable and usually consists of loans receivable and notes receivable, the latter being represented in writing.

Life Insurance (CSV): CSV stands for cash surrender value. You may need to call your insurance agent to obtain the correct figure.

Real Estate: If you own a house, some land, or have an interest in something like a real estate investment trust, you need to determine the fair market value; that may require appraisal by a professional.

Vehicles: For any automobiles, motorcycles, trucks, snowmobiles, motor homes, boats, airplanes, you need to determine the current fair market value. You can probably get these figures from an installment loan officer at your local bank.

Personal Property: Be careful with items in this category. There's a tendency to throw furniture and appliances in at either their cost when you bought them or their replacement cost. Unless you have a precious oriental rug or a valuable silver collection, value your belongings at what they'd bring at a yard sale. Be certain, though, to include things like coin or stamp collections.

Pension Benefits: If you work for an employer, you may have vested rights in a pension plan. Check with your personnel director. Also include any value of IRAs or Keoughs you have.

Business Interests: If you have already started your business, there may be value in the venture. Check with your accountant. If you value it yourself, be very, *very* conservative.

Other Assets: Usually people will list the value of trusts under other assets. Don't list what I call contingent assets; if you're named in rich Aunt Sadie's will, that has no value until her demise. Other categories might include such items as tax rebates due, insurance dividends, profit-sharing.

Add up the assets and put the result under Total Assets. Surprised? Many people are, but before you go off on some spree, remember, we're going to start listing liabilities, which accountants call claims against the assets. Let's start with the right hand column. As with the assets, we aren't going to deal with *contingent* liabilities. For example, you might be a co-maker or co-guarantor on a car loan for your sister, and if she defaults and can't pay, you'll have to. Liability only occurs if she fails to make the payments, and therefore, it doesn't belong on a net worth statement. Make, however, a separate list of any contingent liabilities (co-endorser of a note, a lien against some asset such as real estate) because a bank will ask for that information when you apply for a loan.

> *Notes Payable to Banks:* This category doesn't include either mortgages or car loans but represents a note in writing which is either secured (i.e., backed by an asset of some kind) or unsecured.

> *Amounts Payable to Others:* This might be a loan by your brother-in-law, a credit union loan, or other personal debts.

> *Accounts Due:* Under the first category, *credit cards,* list all open balances on VISA, MasterCard, gasoline credit cards, Sears, Wards, and the like. In the *installment loan* category, total up things like car loans, loans on pleasure vehicles. Do not show items that you pay for a service like telephone or cable TV.

> *Unpaid Taxes:* List any taxes due on both income and property. Pro-rate any property taxes. For instance, if you actually pay real estate taxes on your home at the end of every year, meaning you don't have a tax escrow account, and this is June, put down one-half of the estimated annual tax.

> *Insurance Loans:* If you have borrowed against your life insurance, figure in the total amount you've borrowed. Note that if on the asset side you put down *net* CSV (total CSV less outstanding loans), leave this item blank.

> *Mortgages:* Show the *principal* balance (not any interest) of all mortgages.

> *Other Debts:* This category is a catch-all and includes medical bills, a pledge you have made to a charitable organization, a legal judgment. Again, don't show normal operating expenses here.

Add up all your debts and obligations and put the sum under total liabilities. Next, subtract total liabilities from total assets: the result is your net worth. Then add total liabilities to net worth to give liabilities and net worth which should equal total assets. Now you can celebrate (we hope).

What you just did in arriving at your net worth is to figure out the absolute maximum amount of cash you can lay your hands on if you get rid of everything that you own and owe. The chances of your doing that are next to zero, but you now have an idea of sources you can tap for your business. When I started one of my businesses, I sold off all of my stock, borrowed on my life insurance, and pledged my personal residence as collateral against a business loan. If you're a year or even two away from starting your business, you'll have to update your net worth statement; but once you've done it the first time, subsequent calculations are a piece of cake.

Now that you know something about your net worth, you must estimate monthly living expenses. Determining how much money you need to live on is a vital step, not just an academic exercise. Too many people say to me that to get into their own business they're willing to live in a hovel, eat curds and whey, and drive a 10-year-old car. Although some may make adjustments here and there, most people who adopt a certain lifestyle maintain that lifestyle. You should not put yourself in a position of extreme personal sacrifice. A business should provide a certain standard of living and if it doesn't, you may feel that the whole escapade isn't worth the time and effort. I did say earlier that good entrepreneurs don't pursue personal wealth as an end product, but they do understand economic values. If a business can't pay you a fair salary, then it's not a business, it's a hobby.

The next page is a form to estimate your current monthly expenses. Do it now even though you don't plan to be in business for a while, to give you an idea of your present expenses. In the next chapter I'll show how to do a business plan, and one of the items that goes into the financial part of the plan is how much you'll take from the business. Banks and other financial sources get turned off if you show little or no compensation for yourself; if you don't plan for it in the beginning, you may never get to where you should be financially.

The monthly expenses statement is self-explanatory; remember, however, you'll have to adjust some expenses to get them on a monthly rather than a weekly basis. For instance, if your average food bill is $60 per week, then you need to multiply by 4⅓ or 4.33 to reflect a monthly level:

$$\$60 \times 4.33 = \$260/\text{month}$$

Similarly, if your real estate taxes are $1200 annually, you will need to divide by 12:

$$\frac{\$1200}{12} = \$100/\text{month}$$

Now let's summarize what you've discovered and what it means to your startup. As I said before, your net worth statement will tell you the maximum amount of money you could raise from your personal assets, but you will certainly not use all of it. It's a good idea to earmark which assets will be converted to cash. Once you do this, you will have an amount of money that represents your personal investment in the business. Many people ask how much is needed to start your own business and the answer to that will come when you do your business plan in the next chapter. Obviously the need for capital varies with the type of business, its initial size, and the planned rate of growth. Beginning an accounting practice in your home with some stationery, a business phone, and a few local ads certainly differs from the financial commitments for the startup of a computer manufacturing firm. Also, your own personal needs, as expressed in the monthly expense analysis, will have a direct effect on what you need to take from the business for your support and lifestyle. A business, by the way, should provide three types of financial "return" to the business owner:

1. A fair salary comparable to that of a manager of that kind of business.
2. A return for the risk of enterprise.
3. Sufficient cash flow to fund the business's assets.

Legal Form of the Business

It's a good idea to consider the legal form of your business before you begin full-time operation. It's also important that you consult with your accountant and your attorney on these matters. The form of the business that you select depends on a number of factors:

1. The type of outside financing you need.
2. Tax considerations.
3. The size of the business.
4. Your ultimate plans for the business.
5. Your personal desires.
6. Advice of your accountant and attorney.
7. Laws.

ESTIMATED MONTHLY EXPENSES

Item	Amount
Food	$
Housing	
a. Monthly payment or rent	
b. Taxes	
c. Insurance	
d. Repairs and maintenance	
Clothing	
Auto	
a. Payment	
b. Gasoline	
c. Repairs	
d. Insurance, fees, taxes	
Utilities	
a. Electricity	
b. Heat, hot water (if not electric)	
c. Telephone	
d. Other (water, gas)	
Credit cards (not covered elsewhere)	
Installment and other loans	
Life Insurance	
Travel and entertainment	
Donations	
Medical and dental	
Investment and savings	
Miscellaneous	
TOTAL	$

Let's briefly look at the three common forms of business.

The Sole Proprietorship The sole proprietorship is the most prevalent form of business in the United States. Of the 15 million businesses in existence, about three-fourths of them are proprietorships. They tend to be much smaller in terms of annual receipts than either partnerships or corporations, however. It's by far the simplest form of operation. Write to the Secretary of State in your state capital to see if there are any forms you need to submit; in many states all you need to do is to register your trade name, the name under which you will do business. The reasons for this are two-fold: (1) to be certain that someone else in the state is not already using the name you want, and (2) to avoid having your state government come after you five years later with a bill for back proprietorship taxes, penalties, and interest.

In the eyes of the law and the Internal Revenue Service (IRS), you and the proprietorship are one and the same. It isn't really a form of business at all but merely an extension of you. Suppose you hold yard sales from time to time. Unless you specifically form a partnership or a corporation to conduct this activity, you're functioning as a proprietorship. In a proprietorship, it's usually you alone although your spouse can be a part of it, especially if you file a joint tax return. It often makes a handy vehicle for operating a business while working on a part-time basis.

A proprietorship itself can't raise money. Because you and the business are one, the only way that you can secure outside financing is personally—there can be no limited partners or stockholders.

You can start and stop proprietorships almost at will. There is very little paperwork or legality involved. Because you and the proprietorship are one, you're automatically and personally liable for anything done in the name of the business. If you run a store and someone slips on your floor, any claim for damages will be brought against you as an individual, not against the business. In some states, you must specify legally the fact that you are operating a proprietorship, especially if your own name doesn't appear in the business name. For instance, a typical designation might be

William R. Quinlan
d/b/a Bill's Oil Co.

The "d/b/a" means doing business as. You may use the word company or its abbreviation, but you may not use "Inc.," "Corp.," "Ltd."—those terms are reserved for corporations. Also, a proprietorship ceases to exist if you do: i.e., you die or are unable to carry on business.

Tax regulations change frequently and they can be complex when it comes to business. For a proprietorship, you or your accountant will complete Schedule C of IRS Form 1040. This is merely a schedule summarizing income and expenses. You can obtain a copy of the latest form at your nearest IRS office—check your phone book under "U.S. Government" headings. If the office doesn't have the form, you call the toll-free IRS forms number. One very strong point about proprietorships and taxable income: unless the IRS drastically changes its philosophy, when you operate a proprietorship you pay *personal* taxes on the profit of the business operation regardless of whether or not you took any money out of the business for your own use. This is a very important point. I have encountered a number of people who say, "I don't have to pay any taxes because I didn't earn any money," meaning that they didn't write themselves a check or grab cash out of the drawer. Review what I said before: You and the business are one and the same. If the business earns money, you earn money and have to pay tax on it. As a matter of fact, you may be fined by the IRS if your proprietorship makes money and you don't file quarterly estimated tax statements (Form 1040-ES). Again, check with your accountant or the nearest IRS office for the latest forms and regulations. Also ask the IRS for their free literature for business taxes; I also suggest you obtain a copy of the latest revision of *Small-Time Operator: How to Start Your Own Small Business, Keep Your Books, Pay Your Taxes, & Stay Out of Trouble,* by Bernard Kamoroff, CPA. Bell Springs Publishing, Box 640, Laytonville, CA 95454.

Partnerships formed for the purposes of conducting business ventures are becoming less popular, mainly because they are almost as complicated to form as corporations but possess few of the advantages. A partnership is nothing more

The Partnership

than a venture of two or more proprietors, but most partnerships form these days as a tax advantage for wealthy individuals, to allow them to invest in something—real estate, cattle, freight cars. If you're contemplating a partnership, be certain to get good legal and accounting advice, because it may be far more advantageous to form a corporation. I rarely give out absolute advice, but if you go the partnership route, *NEVER* form a 50-50 partnership with one other individual; make it unbalanced in one direction or another. The 50-50 arrangement almost inevitably leads to unresolved bickering and dissolution, even with a husband-and-wife combination.

A partnership is usually established with the drawing up and execution of a written partnership agreement which, among other things, contains the following information:

> The names and addresses of the partners and the partnership.
> The nature of the business to be conducted.
> The duration of the partnership if it is to have a limited life.
> The amounts of capital initially supplied by each partner, how much money they'll each earn, and how the profits will be distributed.
> The duties of the partners, whether the partners are general partners or limited partners, and whether one is to be a managing partner, the chief executive.
> The procedure by which an existing partner may withdraw or be bought out or a new partner added.
> The way the business can be dissolved, including who gets what if a partner dies or is incapable of participating any longer.

There are two types of partners, general and limited. All general partners participate in the day-to-day operation of the business. They usually supply capital of their own, but they may not. Any general partner may be held personally responsible not only for the actions of the firm as a whole but also for the actions of the other partners individually. A limited (or silent) partner supplies capital only, and doesn't engage in the operation of the business. The word limited comes from the fact that if the partnership gets into a legal hassle, the limited partners are only liable to the extent of the capital they've supplied. Unlike general partners, they can't normally be sued personally.

Partnerships have an advantage over proprietorships by having not only more capital available but also more expertise. One disadvantage is that legally a partnership ceases to exist upon the withdrawal or death of one of the partners. Because this can cause both management and financial upheaval, it's very important these matters be covered in the partnership agreement. Such agreements are usually drawn up by a lawyer.

Partners pay personal taxes on the profit of the partnership whether that profit is distributed in cash or not. If you, as a partner, are entitled to 40 percent of the profits, and the partnership shows a profit of $20,000, you will owe tax on $8,000; this in addition to any salary you receive. The partnership itself doesn't pay taxes; it files Form 1065 (Partnership Return) which is known as an information return. There are no taxes due with this form because each partner files Schedule E of Form 1040 and computes his or her own taxes.

Remember, partnerships are not very common; only 8 percent of businesses choose this legal form of operation. If you do form a partnership, be very certain that you know the reasons behind your action.

The Corporation   Unlike either a proprietorship or a partnership, a corporation is regarded as a legal entity separate from its owners, called stockholders, and its managers, who may or may not be stockholders. The corporation may enter into contracts; it may borrow money; it may break the law; it may be sued. Unless the founder(s) of the corporation specifies to the contrary, a corporation has a perpetual life. It doesn't go out of existence even if its sole stockholder dies.

You have two choices in forming a corporation—you may do it yourself or you may have your attorney do it for you. A corporation must make its application to a particular state but that state doesn't have to be the one in which the corporation operates. If you decide to form it yourself, do so only if you have a reasonably strong background in business. The terminology you have to deal with can be quite strange to those unfamiliar with business.

Let's briefly describe how a corporation operates. First, there are stockholders or owners. Most states allow a corporation to have a single stockholder, who normally will be you. Stockholders put money into a corporation called equity financing, which goes to buy ownership. For instance, if you put $5,000 into your corporation and you're the only one doing so, you own 100 percent of the *stock* of the corporation. If, on the other hand, you put in $3,000 and a friend invests $2,000, you own three-fifths, or 60 percent, and your friend 40 percent. The initial investor(s) is called the founder. The stockholder(s) then elects the directors who normally serve one-year terms on a board of directors. States have different requirements governing the number of directors, but many now allow a single director if there is a single stockholder. At the first official meeting of the board of directors officers are elected: usually, a president, a treasurer, and a secretary or clerk. Again, requirements vary from state to state regarding the number of officers. If you're the founder, the sole stockholder, and the only director, and you use your attorney to form the corporation, it's very common for you to be both president and treasurer, with your lawyer serving as secretary. This makes sense because the secretary (called clerk in some states) is more or less the legal representative of the corporation. For example, if the corporation is sued, the secretary (who is usually designated the "agent of service") will be served the legal papers.

If you're considering forming your own corporation, get a copy of *How to Form Your Own Corporation Without a Lawyer For Under $50* by Ted Nicholas from:

Enterprise Publishing, Inc.
725 Market St.
Wilmington, DE 19801.

This inexpensive book has all the procedures and forms necessary for you to file in the state of Delaware, where corporation formation is relatively easy. The procedure is simple and straightforward, but it will take time to do it.

Once you incorporate in Delaware, you're known as a domestic corporation in Delaware. Because you're not located in that state, you need to designate an agent in Wilmington, the capital. You're also required to file as a foreign corporation in your home state; this requires more fees and more paperwork. Nicholas' book helps you through both those areas. I realize this sounds complicated, but if you want to file yourself, it's simpler and cheaper to go the Delaware route than to make application to your home state without the assistance of a lawyer. Why Delaware? Here are a few reasons:

1. About two-fifths of corporations listed on the New York Stock Exchange and one-third of those on the American Stock Exchange are incorporated in Delaware.
2. There is no minimum *paid-in capital* requirement. Some states require at least $1,000.

3. Several states require the purpose (i.e., the business reason) of the corporation to be specified in restrictive terms. Delaware, in the Certificate of Incorporation, accepts the following:

> The purpose of the corporation is to engage in any lawful act or activity for which corporations may be organized under the general Corporation Law of Delaware.

4. A single individual may be the sole stockholder, all the directors, and all the officers.
5. The annual fee for corporations, called a franchise tax, is comparable with other states. Also, there's no corporate income tax on corporations operating outside of Delaware.
6. In general, the director(s) has (have) a great deal of latitude—fixing the price of the stock, acting by unanimous consent without formal meetings, amending the by-laws.

Consequently, if you want to file yourself, do it in Delaware and use Nicholas's book to do it. The book contains the proper forms for the Certificate of Incorporation, the By-Laws, the first meeting of the director(s), even the Foreign Corporation Certificate for your home state.

If you don't want to do this yourself, you must use an attorney. The advantages to this are:

1. It requires a lot less effort on your part. Most lawyers who form corporations can get the basic information from you—number of stockholders, directors, officers, type of business—in an hour or so.
2. You won't be a domestic corporation in one state and a foreign corporation in your own state. Annual fees will be less.
3. You're securing the services of a professional you may want to become a full team member. Some lawyers don't take kindly to those forming their own company and then requesting legal services.
4. If your attorney also becomes the secretary, he or she will take care of future paperwork with the state.

The only real disadvantage (outside of working with an incompetent or unknowledgeable lawyer) is the expense. Lawyers charge anywhere from $400 to $3,000 to form a corporation; the sad part is that you may be paying a thousand dollars to have the attorney's secretary fill out the forms and mail them.

The choice is really yours. I've gone both routes with equal success. One strong bit of advice if you use a lawyer to form the corporation: very often, entrepreneurs are tight for cash in the beginning and have difficulty justifying a legal fee. Some unscrupulous lawyers may suggest you substitute stock ownership (an equity position in the corporation) for payment of their fee. Under no circumstances should you allow this to happen. Be prepared to pay in cash or don't use one. I've personally seen cases where lawyers grab off 20 to 30 percent of a new corporation; the entrepreneur lives to regret this when the business reaches a substantial size and he or she has to buy out the lawyer for many times what the initial fee would have been.

If you're planning to use the services of an attorney to form the corporation, it's a good idea to bring in an accountant as well because there can be significant tax advantages to the corporate form. Notice I say *can be*. Many people wrongfully assume a corporation is always preferable to, say, a proprietorship for tax purposes, and that's not always so. In addition, tax laws and tax rates change regularly and you shouldn't be spending your time in that arena; leave it to those more qualified, while you stick to your business.

Let's go over a few of the advantages of a corporation. As you have probably noticed, corporations in the United Kingdom have the word "Limited," abbreviated Ltd., after their name. The term comes from the fact that the liability—both financial and personal—on the part of the directors and officers is limited only to the amount of money they have invested in the corporation. This is somewhat true with United States corporations. Why somewhat? We'll start with the issue of personal liability and responsibility. Traditionally in this country, an employee of a corporation, whether the president or the janitor, usually can't be fined or jailed for illegal acts of the corporation as a whole. This, however, seems to be changing. A number of executives have been both fined *and* jailed for price fixing and violations of anti-pollution and safety standards. If you're the only person in your corporation, then you may not have quite the protection that you believe. On the money side of things, you normally expect only to lose your own investment if the business fails, but if you borrow money from a bank and sign personal guarantees for the loan—meaning you'll make good any loss—you'll have to pay the bank yourself if there aren't enough assets in the corporation to cover it. Another way you can get hit is if a dissatisfied stockholder believes you're acting counter to his or her interests. Even though these exceptions to the limited liability concept are rare, they can occur nonetheless. In general, however, there's more protection with the corporate form than with either the proprietorship or partnership.

One of the biggest advantages of the corporation concerns the issue of common stock. Shares of stock may be sold to individuals or groups of individuals such as venture capitalists in order to raise money, and the funds received are not taxable. These shares have value (assuming that the corporation operates profitably) and may be distributed to family members, used for estate planning, pledged as security for a personal loan, and transferred or sold without dissolving the corporation.

A corporation also generally provides a business owner with a tax advantage. Where it doesn't, it's usually a case of an entrepreneur operating a proprietorship so small it has little or no profit. Tax rates (i.e., percentages) increase as taxable income increases, and this is true for individuals as well as corporations. If you operate a proprietorship and have a large profit, it's taxed at a high rate. If you're the sole stockholder of a corporation, you can pay yourself a salary of, say, half the profit that existed in the proprietorship form of business and leave the other half to be taxed at the corporate tax rate. By splitting the amount and dropping both halves into lower tax brackets, you reduce your total tax liability.

A corporation gives you more flexibility when setting up a pension or profit-sharing plan which might be tax deductible. A corporation can lease the automobile you use and deduct the lease payments. As we said before, it's important to get good advice from your accountant.

However, there are disadvantages to a corporation:

1. There's a lot more paperwork, especially compared to a proprietorship. If you're the only employee of your corporation, you pay yourself a salary and that means more records; it also entails more expense—employer's portion of social security, state unemployment tax, federal unemployment tax. You must file quarterly 941 reports to the IRS, annual wage statements to social security, franchise tax statement to your state, data to the Bureau of the Census on the nature of your business.
2. Unlike a proprietorship, you must be concerned with two tax returns—personal and corporate. Even if you can skillfully do the individual 1040

form, you will probably not be proficient with the corporate 1120 form; that means paying an accountant to do it for you.

3. If you pay dividends on the stock, they're taxed twice, once to the corporation and once to you. Nor can you pay yourself a small salary and leave large profits within the corporation. The IRS calls that "improperly retained earnings;" they may fine you and make you pay out those earnings to yourself in the form of dividends which will also be taxed.

4. The general public has some strange ideas about corporations. Many people believe a corporation has an infinite amount of money even if it's just you, so you may be asked to donate to all manner of local causes and charities.

There are two more important options available to corporations, and both require written action by the board of directors. The first is what's known as a Subchapter S corporation. When the directors choose Sub S, they allow the corporation to act as a partnership for tax purposes. The profit or loss of the corporation is passed on to the stockholders themselves. Normally, the directors elect the Sub S option while the corporation is losing money, which it often does during its early years because of high startup expenses and low sales. When the corporation becomes profitable, the directors then de-elect the option. You need to obtain IRS Form 2553 (Election by a Small Business Corporation—As to taxable status under Subchapter S of the Internal Revenue Code) and file two copies with the nearest IRS center. All stockholders—and the company cannot have more than 15*—must consent and sign the form. The election (or de-election) is then noted in the corporate records. It's a good idea to keep copies of the 2553 form as well.

The second decision actually complements the Subchapter S election, and the two often go hand in hand. If you buy stock in some big company like IBM or Exxon and that company goes bust, the stock is worthless. You can't deduct all of your loss for income tax purposes because the IRS says you have a *capital* loss—and that kind of loss is subject to limitations and restrictions. Section 1244 of the Internal Revenue Code, however, permits stockholders (i.e., people, not other corporations or trusts) to deduct up to $25,000 ($50,000 for a joint return) from *ordinary* income for stock-related losses of a small business corporation, as long as the directors have put this legal principle into effect. The 1244 option is usually done at the time of the formation of the corporation by making a standard one-page notation to the minutes of the first meeting of the directors. You don't have to file anything with the IRS.

The Sub S and the 1244 options are both attractive to outside investors. As long as the corporation meets certain minimum standards—having only one class of stock owned by less than 15 stockholders, all of whom are individuals and U.S. citizens—it may qualify for Sub S. Most of those that qualify for Sub S qualify under Section 1244. If you're using an attorney to form a corporation, be sure to mention these options. If your attorney looks at you and says, "Huh?" find a new lawyer.

Which Way to Go?   I'll bet some of you wonder why you can't just be in business without all this folderol of equity and directors and Subchapter S. Well, you can be if you choose the sole proprietorship route. It's simple and well-traveled. The problem is money. In the first place, as the proprietorship gets more and more profitable, that profit is taxed at personal rates and it doesn't take long to get into the top brackets where taxes are stiff. Second, a proprietorship is limited to

---

* These stockholders must also be people, not other corporations, and these people must be United States citizens.

borrowing money on the part of the proprietor. My advice is to operate initially as a proprietorship, especially if you're going to do it part-time and by yourself. If you're full-time and by yourself, give serious thought to the corporate form. If you're going to open the doors to your business with employees, definitely form a corporation. You notice I haven't mentioned partnerships. That's deliberate—I usually don't recommend them.

Selecting Your Advisors

Your primary advisors are your accountant and your attorney. I can't stress strongly enough how important they are, especially if your knowledge of financial matters and business law is limited. Yes, they're expensive; their rates may run to $100 per hour, but if they save you money in the long run, their fees are well worth it. Of course, the opposite is true as well; poor ones waste both your time and your money and may even create problems for you. Ask other small business owners, the local chamber of commerce, your bank, before you hire. Look for individuals in sole practice or with very small firms. Don't automatically go to the largest accounting or law firm; you may pay more and get less personal service. When you visit your accountant and attorney, tell them about you and your business idea. Normally the first visit to these professionals is free; if either wants to charge, I think you'd be wise to keep looking. *You* interview *them*. Ask about their past experiences with startups, especially the lawyer's. Inquire about their rates. If you are satisfied with a person's technical competence, you should also like him as a person.

Your Accountant

Many people confuse bookkeeping with accounting. The former consists primarily of writing numbers in such a way that proper records may be kept. Bookkeeping is an intermediate step in the creation of the financial statements used to analyze the performance of the business. I recommend you do your own books. You can use the forms and methods suggested in Kamaroff's *Small Time Operator* referenced earlier in this chapter; you can purchase one of the "Ideal" books from your local bookstore or office supply business; or, if your business is very simple, your checkbook can suffice as long as you carefully record where your business receipts come from and what your checks (disbursements) are written for. Don't hire an accountant to do bookkeeping.

I highly recommend you look for a *certified public accountant* or CPA. Yes, you'll pay more but you'll get an individual with a broader background and more expertise. Most states who license CPAs require:

1. A college degree with a minimum of 24 hours (usually eight courses) of accounting subjects.
2. A certain amount of time spent working for a public accounting firm.
3. Several examinations.

A good CPA usually recommends you begin by having him or her prepare your annual tax reports, both personal and business. When they do your taxes, they will probably want to review the business with you. In this early period, a CPA can also help you with the preparation of financial statements for a bank loan. As your business grows, your accountant can furnish you with additional financial reports: quarterly statements at first, then monthly statements.

My best advice is: listen to your accountant. You're paying for what this professional knows and is able to tell you. Notice that I said listen. That does not necessarily mean obey. The one problem I find with accountants is that they'll often give advice only from a financial standpoint, and that's not necessarily the same as from a business view. For example, suppose your accountant tells you to raise your prices. If you've done careful marketing research, including competitive analysis, and have established your prices for good *marketing* reasons, then raising your prices may not necessarily be good advice.

Your Attorney   Use the same degree of care when selecting an attorney. Find one who is knowledgeable and personable; someone you can ask a question and get a reasonably straight answer from. Lawyers, like accountants, tend to be a conservative lot, but this is probably an advantage. When it's you and your business operating in a country that passes 30,000 laws a year, you don't want to be dealing with a gunslinger. When you look for an attorney, be sure to find one with business experience. You don't want someone who specializes in domestic suits and divorces or in criminal law. If you can't find one by word of mouth, write to the state bar association or go to a library and ask to see a copy of *Martindale-Hubbel,* a national directory of lawyers and law firms showing professional specialties.

Expect to use an attorney to form a corporation, draft a partnership agreement, examine legal documents (e.g., a lease), and draw up employment contracts. If you're going to be in business, you can also eventually expect to be a party to a court action, whether you initiate it or not. A lawyer can't *prevent* you from being sued, but you'll need one if you're named in a suit of any kind.

Finally, don't expect a good attorney to make decisions for you. The good ones present options and advise what they believe to be your best course of action, but they won't do it for you. Also, be careful about taking *business* advice from a lawyer; most of them understand the legal implications of business but few understand business itself.

Other Advisors   Anyone can, of course, be an advisor to you, including your mother. If the lady has business experience, fine, but if not, you'll find out all over again what being polite really means. What I mean by advisors are people who have an interest in small business. One very trusted advisor is your banker. Get one thing straight from the beginning: Bankers aren't the enemy. While it's true that most bankers have never been through what you're doing, they talk with many would-be entrepreneurs and observe many small businesses. Because they have been involved in some business failures, they may have some very valuable advice for you, especially about the local climate.

Visit your local Small Business Administration (SBA) office and ask to see one of the management assistance officers. Go over your ideas with that person and listen to what he or she has to say. Remember, you don't have to follow their advice but you should pay attention. The officer might recommend that you use someone from either their SCORE (Service Corps of Retired Executives) or ACE (Active Corps of Executives) programs. The service of these people is free but you have to pay their travel expenses. Be a little careful with SCORE and ACE representatives; some of them, according to some rather sad tales, have given well-meaning but poor advice. One SBA program that seems to work well is the establishment of Small Business Development Centers (SBDCs) at local colleges and universities. In some instances the advice you get from consultants at SBDCs is free; in other cases you'll pay a fee.

There are also private consultants who specialize in small business. They charge from $25 to $60 per hour, and, unlike lawyers or CPAs, are under no minimum educational or experience requirements and have taken no qualifying exams. If you use consultants, be certain to check them out in advance. If they're good at what they do, buying a few hours of their time is well worth what you spend.

Another important advisor is a good business insurance agent. You may not need any insurance to begin with, especially if you are starting out on a part-time basis, but as time goes on and your business grows, you may need to consider insurance against liability (both for accidents on the premises and for product liability), fire and theft, business interruption, and medical costs. If there are others starting the business with you, you may want to consider key person insurance. This is a policy that pays money to the business if a key person dies or is incapacitated. You may also want to use insurance plans to create pension benefits.

Don't overlook other business owners as advisors. Most of them will feel flattered to talk with you, even those in the same kind of business. If you find some uncooperative owners, politely excuse yourself. Chances are those people are operating out of some kind of fear and you wouldn't find their advice helpful anyway.

Regarding advisors: Some entrepreneurs try to do everything themselves—form their corporation, set up their books, select their own types of insurance coverage. While I have seen businesses in which the business owner can do all these successfully—a small service business, for example—those situations are the exception rather than the rule. I urge you to use advisors, especially if you have little or no experience in the area in question. These people will more than likely save you far more than their services will cost. I think there is a misconception on the part of some entrepreneurs that they will save money doing everything themselves; my question to them is, "What's your own time worth?"

Now we'll move into an area where you might need some additional outside help—marketing research.

Simple Marketing Research

If you don't have a business idea that meets the demands of the market, raising lots of money won't do anything but prolong the ultimate demise of the venture. At that point you'll also be broke.

There are three very simple things to do before you make any serious attempts to get your business going:

1. Use published data and statistics to estimate the potential size of the business and how much you can earn.
2. Do a brief market survey.
3. Analyze competition.

Let's take one at a time.

There are lots of data to help you estimate how large an "average" business of the kind you're considering should be. This isn't true for every kind of business, however. Published data also doesn't work very well if you're going to start your operation in your home on a part-time basis. You may also be thinking about a business that doesn't easily fit into some well-defined category. I have three uncles who, once upon a time, opened up a gas station that was also a liquor store and a parakeet shop. It was probably the only business of its kind in the world. It also failed.

However, most of you will be able to find some usable information if you spend some time looking around. I suggest you visit three places: a large library with a good business reference section, and your nearest SBA and U.S. Department of Commerce offices. Locations of these government offices are listed in the Appendix. Talk to people at all three places and tell them what you're trying to do. Let's run through a brief example to demonstrate what I'm talking about.

Jack wants to open a small sporting goods store in his town. Certainly he'll do some business because there are other sporting goods stores in his town already; but the question is, how much business—annual sales—can he expect to do? The parallel question is: can he make enough of a living to meet his needs as expressed by his estimated monthly expenses?

The first thing Jack does to find out what an average sporting goods store annually grosses in his locale is to call, write, and visit the departments of state government that collect statistics on businesses within the state, usually the office of economic development. This takes a little effort to track down, but many state governments have an information number to direct people to the proper agency. Another route he uses is to get a copy of the latest *Census of Retail Trade* for his state. This document is found in large libraries, at the nearest U.S. Department of Commerce field offices (See Appendix B for a list of these offices), or it can be purchased from a U.S. Government bookstore or directly from the Superintendent of Documents, U.S. Government Printing Office, Washington, DC 20402. He needs to find the county in which his store will be located and then the listing for SIC* code 5941, which is the designation for "sporting goods stores and bicycle shops." Sometimes the Department of Commerce doesn't report sales data for a particular kind of business because there are too few of them, and the reporting of the combined sales is "withheld to avoid disclosing data for individual companies." If such is the case, Jack will have to use statewide data.

Let's assume he's lucky and finds that in his county there are seven sporting goods stores with combined sales of $1,750,000. The average sales per store, then, is

$$\frac{\$1,750,000}{7} = \$250,000$$

But Jack will be opening a new store, the eighth one. So if people in the area spend no more money on sporting goods, he can expect his sales to be

$$\frac{\$1,750,000}{8} = \$218,750$$

There's one more calculation Jack does. In one of the tables in the Census of Retail Trade he finds the per capita (per person regardless of age) expenditure statewide for sporting goods. Let's suppppose he discovers it's $50.00. Now, if he knows the population of the buying area (city, county) that he'll be operating in, he'll have another check on his business level. We'll assume that he's locating in a medium-size town of 39,000 people. Therefore, the expected purchases of sporting goods in total for that town is

$$\$50 \times 39,000 = \$1,950,000$$

and with eight stores in existence, the average *could* be

$$\frac{\$1,950,000}{8} = \$243,750.$$

Why is this figure higher than the $218,750 he calculated earlier? Well, maybe some people in that town buy their sporting goods elsewhere. If this is the case, he might be able to capture some of this "lost" business.

---

* Standard Industrial Classification—a four-digit number assigned to businesses by the Department of Commerce.

To get an operating figure, let's imagine that Jack takes a simple average of the two numbers:

$$\frac{\$218,750 + \$243,750}{2} = \$231,250$$

Next, Jack wants to figure out if a sporting goods store of that size can support him. He goes to a library or bank and gets the latest copy of *Annual Statement Studies,* published yearly by Robert Morris Associates, Philadelphia Bank Building, Philadelphia, PA 19107. By looking up SIC 5941, he discovers that the median figure for "officers compensation/sales" is 5.1 percent. For planning purposes, he can then estimate his own earnings at

$$0.051 \times \$231,250 = \$11,800.$$

Always remember, we're dealing with averages. Of the seven sporting goods stores in his town, probably none are average. Some are small and some are large. There may be one or two large discount department stores with sporting goods sections whose data are not reported. Jack personally visits every store that sells any kind of sporting goods.

You may find that the business you're contemplating can't be found in the government data. In that case, find out if there's a professional association for that type of business by checking the *Encyclopedia of Associations.* Also find out which magazines are read by people in that business; visit your library and ask for *Standard Rate and Data Service—Periodicals* or the *Ayer Directory of Newspapers and Periodicals.* Contact the appropriate magazine editors and ask if any articles have been written or any studies done on business size and owner's compensation for your type of business. Consider subscribing to one or two of the periodicals published for business owners in the industry you are considering.

One other technique to consider is a marketing survey, especially if you can't find much information about the business you're contemplating. The purpose of such a survey is to find out if your business ideas are sound, and how much people are willing to spend for your product or service. If you give a little thought to the questions you ask, you get enough data to make estimates. You can call people on the phone, interview them in person, or mail out questionnaires. The problem with the latter is response; you can expect about a 10 to 20 percent return. To get enough meaningful information, you'll have to mail out at least 1,000 questionnaires and need to provide return postage with a business reply envelope. You can get names from a mailing list company (see your Yellow Pages), but most of them have a minimum order of 5,000 names that will cost around $300. If you do it this way, it will cost the following:

Postage: $0.20 × 5,000	$1,000
Return postage: 15% × 5,000 × $0.25	188
Printing costs: $0.25 × 5,000	1,250
Mailing list rental	300
TOTAL	$2,738

That's pretty expensive. If you mail out only 1,000 questionnaires, you'll probably have to compile your own mailing list from your city directory at the library. You might be fortunate enough to borrow a list from someone (the YMCA, a local charity) but the list might be biased. Obviously if you borrow the membership list from your local country club, you get people with incomes higher than the average and this might lead you to false conclusions if you try to draw parallels to the population as a whole.

If you're selling your product or service to a customer group different from the general population—to businesses, for example—it's obvious that you'll need to survey that group.

Let's talk a bit about other ways to do surveys—by telephone and in person. I'll use two actual examples done by some friends and former students of mine. Remember, we're not talking about surveys and marketing research as some kind of academic exercise; this book is about finding seed money and no bank or other lender is going to listen to you for very long if you can't answer the obvious question, "What makes you think this business is going to make it?" You're going to make it by having enough customers spending enough money at your business. Period. Successful marketing, the major key to financing and operating a successful business, can be summed up like this:

> You find out what people want and give them more of it. You find out what people don't want and give them none of it.

Debra Horton did a marketing survey for a soda shop and candy store that would cater primarily to kids: elementary, junior high, and high school students. If you're going to sell things to kids, you'd better know what kids want and what they'll spend their money on. So Debra surveyed one group of students ages 7–12 and a second group ages 12–18 in Brattleboro, Vermont. The two questionnaire forms are on the next page.

What she discovered is summarized below. Debra estimated that, because of the store's proposed location, the kids would spend one-fifth (20 percent) of their ice cream and candy money there.

	7–12 Group	12–18 Group
A. Average weekly spending money	$3.00	$16.60
B. Percent spent on sodas, candy, ice cream, cigarettes, arcade games	73%	59%
C. Money spent on sodas, etc. (A times B)	$2.19	$9.79
D. Money spent in this store (1/5 of C).	$0.44	$1.96
E. Estimated number of kids	450	350
F. Expected weekly store income (D times E)	$198.00	$685.58

To get the expected annual gross, she simply added the weekly incomes from the two age groups and multiplied by 52 weeks:

$$(\$198.00 + \$685.58) \times 52 = \$45,946$$

Considering the cost of ice cream and sundries, rent, utilities, equipment, a gross of $45,000 annually doesn't leave much left for the owner. The other problem Debra discovered was that the business was seasonal with low sales in the winter. Naturally, some adults would use the store, but probably not enough to increase sales dramatically.

1. What is your age?
2. How often do you go to town?
3. How much money do you spend a week?
4. What do you spend most of your money on?
5. What is your favorite treat?
6. How much do you spend on soda a week?
7. How much do you spend on candy a week?   How often?
8. How much of your candy money is for candy bars?
9. How much of your candy money is for penny candy?
10. How much do you spend on holiday candy?   Which holidays?
11. How much do you spend on ice cream in the winter?   How often?
12. How much do you spend on ice cream in the summer?   How often?
13. How much of your ice cream money is for cones in the winter?
14. How much of your ice cream money is for cones in the summer?
15. How much do you spend on sundaes in the winter?   How often?
16. How much do you spend on sundaes in the summer?   How often?
17. Besides cones and sundaes, what other kinds of frozen treats do you buy?   How often?
18. Do you go to video arcade game stores?*   How often?
    a. What time do you usually go in the winter?
        _____ o'clock to _____ o'clock
    b. What time do you usually go in the summer?
        _____ o'clock to _____ o'clock
    c. Do you often stay until closing in winter?   In summer?
19. Is there anything you would like to buy but can't find in Brattleboro?

1. What's your age?
2. How often do you go to town?
3. Where do you go in town?
4. Do you usually go with friends or family?
5. How much spending money for personal use do you average a week?
6. Where do you make most of your purchases?
7. How much do you spend on cigarettes?   How often?
8. How much do you spend on soda?   How often?
9. How much do you spend on candy?   How often?
10. How much of that spending is on bar candy?
11. How much of that spending is on penny candy?
12. How much do you spend on holiday candy?   How often?
13. How much do you spend on ice cream in winter?   How often?
14. How much do you spend on ice cream in summer?   How often?
15. How much do you spend on cones in winter?   How often?
16. How much do you spend on cones in summer?   How often?
17. How much do you spend on sundaes in winter?   How often?
18. How much do you spend on sundaes in summer?   How often?
19. If not cones or sundaes, what other frozen sweets?
20. How much do you think you spend in video arcades each time you go?*   How often?
    a. What time would you usually go in winter?
        _____ o'clock to _____ o'clock
    b. Do you often stay until closing in winter? In summer?
21. Is there any product you would like to buy but can't find in Brattleboro?

---

* This question appears on both questionnaires primarily to discover times when youngsters and teenagers are most likely to be in town with money to spend.

The other survey was done by Don Pasha and Brad Silver; the purpose was to discover if a store selling frozen food, canned goods, and detergents in case lots could be viable in Brattleboro, Vermont. There is no other such establishment of this kind in the area. One page of the phone book was chosen at random and successful calls were made to 53 households. Not everyone responded to every question.

Responses

1. Purchasing in bulk lots, on a cash and carry basis, thereby saving 10 to 30 percent:
   44 households—YES
   9 households—NO
2. Saving an additional 1 to 2 percent by paying in advance:
   29 households YES or MAYBE
   (A little over ½ answered "maybe," depending on the reliability of the company over a "trial period.")
   24 households—NO
3. Number of people in household: Average of 3.4 people per household
4. Ownership of a freezer:
   31 households—YES
   22 households—NO
5. Approximate weekly cost of groceries and cleaning supplies:
   Average of $75 to $100
6. Purchasing of generic-label items:
   29 households—YES
   (Majority is less than ½ of total bill.)
   20 households—NO
7. Preference of price or quality:
   3 households—PRICE
   32 households—QUALITY
   18 households—BOTH

Product Preference

1. Purchase of frozen orange juice:
   37 households—YES
   11 households—NO
   Favorite brands: Minute Maid, Tree Sweet.
2. Type of laundry detergent:
   Tide—10 households
   Dash—6 households
   Wisk—5 households
   Cheer—4 households
   Misc. brands—balance of households
3. Purchase of frozen vegetables:
   33 households—YES
   11 households—NO
   Most mentioned types: peas, green beans, broccoli, corn. Favorite brands: Birds Eye, Green Giant.
4. Purchase of frozen dinners:
   36 households—YES
   11 households—NO
   Favorite brands: Swanson (including Hungry Man Dinners), "house" brand meat pies, Weight Watchers.
5. Purchase of canned tuna:
   38 households—YES
   9 households—NO
   Favorite brands: Bumble Bee, Starkist, Geisha. (Tuna packed in water is preferred by most households.)

The survey shows that households of 4 or more people have a 90 percent probability of owning a freezer, and all who do own a freezer responded with a yes or maybe to using the service. While only 25 percent of the households surveyed are willing to pay in advance, another 25 percent are interested in doing so, but prefer to wait until the company has established reliability.

Frozen orange juice is purchased by nearly 80 percent of the households surveyed. Minute Maid and Tree Sweet are the brands most frequently mentioned.

All of the households of 3 or more people buy frozen vegetables, and 50 percent of those with a brand preference choose Birds Eye or Green Giant. All others usually choose a "house" brand. Frozen vegetables most frequently purchased are peas, green beans, broccoli, and corn.

Nearly 80 percent of all households surveyed purchase some type of frozen dinner or entree, with Swanson Hungry Man Dinners named most frequently and "house" brand meat pies purchased regularly. Also named were Buitoni Italian dishes, Green Giant entrees, and Taste-O-Sea Seafood Platters, as well as Weight Watchers dinners. Several people also mentioned frozen pizzas.

Canned tuna is purchased by 80 percent of the households, and they prefer it to be packed in water.

A variety of laundry detergents was mentioned by the households surveyed, but Tide has the largest usage (20 percent of the households). Others mentioned several times were Dash, Wisk, and Cheer.

Let's see what we can do with the survey data when put beside some easy-to-obtain government statistics:

1. In the U.S. Department of Commerce's *1982 U.S. Industrial Outlook,* D&B determined that so-called no frill operations account for 5 percent of retail food sales.
2. The 1980 U.S. Census data for Windham County, Vermont, shows that there are 13,840 households with an average of 2.6 persons per household.

Going back to the survey data we find that

1. 83 percent (44 out of 53) of the households surveyed said that they would purchase in bulk lots.
2. There were 3.4 persons per household in the 53 that were questioned.
3. The respondents said their weekly food bill was $75 to $100.

Before beginning an analysis, let me caution you regarding two areas. In the first place, a sample of 53 households isn't very large. A survey of several hundred would yield more reliable data. But we're looking for general indications—whether the business is viable or not—not trying for exactness the way large consumer products companies like Procter & Gamble do (and even they, with their rooms full of MBAs and huge computers, stub their toes from time to time). Secondly, when people are surveyed by phone, they're more likely to answer "yes" to any questions about whether or not they will buy something. The real test is when they reach for their wallet. With that in mind, let's knock the 83 percent "yes" answers down to 75 percent. One more figure that should be adjusted is the 5 percent no frill retail food expenditures, because not all of those establishments offer case lots; we'll cut it in half to 2.5 percent.

We'll start with the household count. If there are 13,840 households and we can expect 75 percent of them to buy something, we have a potential market of

$$0.75 \times 13,840 = 10,380 \text{ households.}$$

The weekly food bill range is $75 to $100 and we'll use the lower figure to be conservative; but we have to adjust that figure because our sample had more people per household (3.4) than what the Census data shows (2.6). We'll reduce the $75 by the ratio of 2.6 to 3.4:

$$\frac{2.6}{3.4} \times \$75 = \$57 \text{ per week per household}$$

We said we will use 2.5 percent of food costs, so the average amount of money per household that could be expected to be spent in our proposed business is:

$$.025 \times \$57 = \$1.43$$

(Remember there are no other case lot operations in existence.) If we multiply the $1.43 by the number of households

$$\$1.43 \times 10,380 = \$14,843$$

we have the expected total weekly expenditure. By multiplying this by 52, we have the annual sales:

$$52 \times \$14,843 = \$771,836$$

Over three-quarters of a million dollars per year sounds like a lot of money, but food stores don't work on a large margin because the cost of what they sell is high compared to other businesses. Checking again with Robert Morris's *Annual Statement Studies,* we find that the average compensation for food store owners is 1.8 percent. Our new owner can expect to make:

$$.018 \times \$771,836 = \$13,893 \text{ per year}$$

The final piece of marketing research deals with a study of competitors. Visit your competitors if at all possible. Ask others what they think. The form on the facing page will help you record and analyze competitive information. Make copies of the form if necessary.

Timing   This is a simple exercise but it may take you a few hours to complete it. You're going to figure out what you're going to do and when. The various activities that you'll be engaged in—marketing research, writing the business plan, talking to banks—are up to you, but plan from today until the time you open your business for real. That overall time span can be a few weeks, several months, or even a couple of years, depending on a host of factors like how far along you are right now, how complex the business is, how much capital you have. I realize there are unknowns for you. If you've never written a business plan, for example, you might not have much of an idea of how long it will take. A week? A month? Six months? But give it your best estimate nonetheless.

On the pages 40 and 41 I've given a sample schedule for a hypothetical retail business, as well as a blank form covering a 24-month period. If the format isn't to your liking, make up your own; but, for goodness sake, do it. On the sample you notice that some activities take place over time—like four months to write the business plan—and others simply happen, like quitting your job. Also, you can see that some activities overlap.

After a fairly long chapter, you're now ready to take the first real step toward getting your seed money—the preparation of your business plan.

COMPETITIVE ANALYSIS FORM

Business Name _____ Date _____

Address _____

Owner's Name _____

Ratings (use check marks)

	Excellent	Good	Fair	Poor	Doesn't Apply
1. Location					
2. Parking					
3. General Appearance a. Outside b. Inside					
4. Courtesy					
5. Quality					
6. Prices					
7. Credit Policy					
8. Reputation/Image					
9. Availability of Merchandise					
10. Selection of Merchandise					
11. Customer Service					
12. Overall Impression					

List Competitor's Strong Points

List Competitor's Weak Points

Comments

Activity

1. Read and Study
2. Course in Small Business
3. Visit SBA Office
4. Analyze Self
5. Figure Personal Finances
6. Pick Lawyer
7. Pick Accountant
8. Do Marketing Research
9. Write Business Plan
10. Visit Banks
11. Analyze Locations
12. See Insurance Agent
13. Talk with Suppliers
14. Pick Location
15. Quit Job
16. Do Initial Advertising
17. Complete Financing
18. Hire Clerk
19. Stock Shelves
20. Open Doors

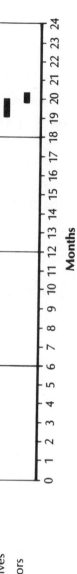

Months

0 1 2 3 4 5 6 7 8 9 10 11 12 13 14 15 16 17 18 19 20 21 22 23 24

Your Business Plan

CHAPTER
Four

Now you're really getting serious. You don't put the time, sweat, tears, and effort behind the preparation of a business plan if you aren't relatively certain you're going to go through with it. *Never* go after seed money without a prospectus, the term used by the financial community for a business plan designed to raise money. Before we begin the building process, however, I want to give you some background.

Purposes of a Plan

A business plan has two basic purposes, one internal and the other external. The internal purpose is the way you'll run the business for the next three to five years. Its preparation forces you to check all the data required to understand and operate the business and to make projections into the future. Then when the business is actually operating, you can check your progress against what you said you would do in your business plan. The external purpose is to raise money—whether it's a few grand from Uncle Harold, a significant amount from a group of private investors, or a loan from a commercial bank. So the plan is also a prospectus. Your chances of raising money without a plan are slim. As a matter of fact, if you take in investment (equity) money from private, unsophisticated citizens, you stand a chance of running afoul of state or federal securities laws if you don't provide sufficient information about the nature of their investment. In fact, some business attorneys advise putting actual warnings in the prospectus regarding the degree of risk startup investors face.

Advantages to Planning

Reduction of Risk. Remember, good entrepreneurs are not dice-throwers. They don't take outrageous risks. By preparing a plan, you reduce your risk because you work things out in advance. Naturally you won't be able to foresee everything that can happen in the future, but you can work through the major events.

Few Surprises. The small business world is a highly technical and complex one. The days of a simple Mom 'n Pop operation circa 1950 are over. Running a business without a plan is like driving a car without paying attention either to the rules of the road or to where you're going. There's an old saw that says if you have no destination, then any road will take you there. I

42

add, if you have no destination, you'll never know when you get there either. People who run businesses without a plan very often see themselves as victims—victims of the economy, competition, the government, their customers, the bank.

Establishes Methodology. Successful businesses today are run according to method. Once you complete your very first business plan, you establish important business methodology. Planning is a learning experience and you get better at it as time goes by. Your first business plan probably won't be your last.

Sets Up Financing. As we'll see as we go along, the business plan establishes in advance how much money you need. It gives your financing sources some reasonable assumptions about why you're asking for the money and how the loan will be repaid or what return an investor will realize (in the case of equity funds).

Many people don't realize there are two systems of logic behind a business plan. The first is overall logic and it looks like this:

The Logic of Planning

```
          ┌──────────────────┐
          │  Starting Point  │
          └──────────────────┘
                   │
                   ▼
          ┌──────────────────┐
  ┌──────▶│      Goals       │
  │       └──────────────────┘
  │                │
  │                ▼
  │       ┌──────────────────┐
Feedback  │       Plan       │
  │       └──────────────────┘
  │                │
  │                ▼
  │       ┌──────────────────┐
  └───────│   Actualities    │
          └──────────────────┘
```

Your starting point is where you are *right now*. It's not where you think you should be. It consists of your present skills and everything else you have to work with. The goals are where you want to go: the products or services you will offer, what your sales and profits will be, how much money you want to raise. The plan is the vehicle to help you reach those goals. Actualities are events occurring in the future; they either occur the way you planned them or they don't. If they don't, you use what you learn to adjust the goals, then there's a new plan, and so on: plan and adjust, plan and adjust.

The other type of logic deals with the technical side of things. I see beginners and even some knowledgeable business owners grab an accounting form and fill it with all kinds of future projections regarding sales, expenses, and income (profit). You can't make valid financial forecasts about sales levels until you address the marketing aspects of the business. That's why we emphasized marketing research in the last chapter. If you can't show where the sales are coming from—customers—all the work put into the financial section is for naught. Everyone knows financial projections are only best guesses and that's all the more reason to analyze the market first. If you don't, how can you answer the banker's or potential investors' question, "Where did you get these numbers from?"

Preparatory Steps   Although it's not necessary to have everything totally settled before you prepare a business plan, you should be able to complete the checklist below.

To begin, you need a pencil (a pen if you're really confident) and a calculator. We're going to go through a typical business plan step by step. The separate workbook contains blank forms in the same order as these explanations. You can use the workbook to prepare the rough draft of your plan as we go along. The final plan is typed in an attractive, professional manner. Yes, neatness does count. (There also is a sample business plan for a manufacturing startup in Appendix C.)

One thing to be aware of right off the bat is that there's no such thing as *the*

PREPARATORY CHECKLIST

Item	Yes	No	In Progress*	Not Applicable
1. Prepared my net worth statement and personal budget.				
2. Picked a name for the business.				
3. Selected a location.				
4. Conducted initial marketing research.				
5. Picked the legal form of the business.				
6. Formed the corporation.				
7. Selected my advisors:				
a. Accountant				
b. Attorney				
c. Consultant				
d. Insurance Agency				
e. Advertising Agency				
8. Checked with my town and state for appropriate licenses and taxes.				
9. Interviewed prospective employees.				
10. Lined up vendors for:				
a. Office supplies				
b. Equipment				
c. Inventory				
d. Other supplies				

* You might also want to note when the item will be completed.

format for a business plan. I've written about 25 plans myself, read hundreds, and have never seen any two the same. This is only a suggested format; if other items occur to you, by all means include them. Don't add material just to give the plan bulk, though; the pros will spot it.

One last word of advice: *You* do the plan. Don't have a consultant do it for you because then it's the consultant's plan and not yours. I'm not against getting help or having someone check over your material. As a matter of fact, it's a good idea to work on the financial section with the aid of your accountant; but remember, it's your plan and your business.

We'll use the following outline in both the explanatory part and the workbook part of the rest of this chapter.

Business Plan—Outline

Title Page
Summary and Purpose (optional)
Table of Contents

I. The Business
   A. Business Description
      1. Name
      2. Location
      3. Physical facilities
   B. Products or Services
      1. Description of product line
      2. Proprietary considerations
   C. Management Plan
      1. Organizational form and structure
      2. Resumés of key people
      3. Staffing plan
      4. Supporting services
   D. Operations Plan
      1. Facilities and equipment
      2. Plans for growth and expansion
      3. Overall schedule
      4. Process description
   E. Risks (optional)

II. Marketing Plan
   A. Marketing Research
      1. Description of market
      2. Industry trends
      3. Target market
      4. Competition
   B. Objectives and Strategy
   C. Pricing Policy
   D. Sales Terms
   E. Method of Sales and Distribution
   F. Customer Service
   G. Advertising and Promotion
   H. Forecasts

III. Financial Data
   A. Proposal
   B. Use of Proceeds

    C. Opening Day Balance Sheet
    D. Cash Flow Projections
    E. Pro Forma Income Statements
    F. Breakeven Analysis

IV. Appendices

Remember, this is a suggested outline and may contain much more than you need in your plan. Some people ask me how long a typical plan should be. Naturally, that depends on the nature of the business and the form of financing desired. For a simple startup like a service, a 10-page plan might be fine. More complex plans are prospectuses written for businesses with fairly large stock offerings and can run to over 100 pages.

Business Plan—Content

TITLE PAGE. This is the blank title page beginning the workbook for the business plan. Notice the remark in parentheses. If you're going to have your plan typed directly from the workbook pages, be sure to scratch out any comments found in parentheses; they're meant only as clarifying notes for you.

SUMMARY AND PURPOSE.

These two are optional. If your plan is relatively simple and straightforward, don't bother. If you plan is more complex, especially if it's going to be given to private investors, venture capitalists, or an SBIC (Small Business Investment Corporation), it's a good idea to include both a summary and a purpose. The summary is usually two to four paragraphs and covers the items shown on the worksheet. Again, remember to remove all parenthetical comments prior to final typing.

Use the purpose section only if you're seeking equity (investment) financing from individuals or organizations that will be stockholders. A typical purpose statement reads:

> The purpose of this prospectus is to raise $30,000 in equity capital. Shares of stock in the XYZ Corporation are available at $10.00 per share, with 3,000 shares offered. Minimum investment is $2,000 (200 shares at $10.00 per share).

Sometimes the equity statement is combined with a debt statement as well. If this were the case in the example above, another sentence would declare:

> In addition, XYZ Corporation is seeking debt financing of $25,000 at currently existing commercial loan rates.

A word of caution about equity financing: get help from an attorney experienced in private stock offerings, a business consultant, an SBA management assistance officer, or a qualified banker. Securities laws are lengthy and they do change. How can you figure out how much money you need until you complete the financial projections of income and expenses later in the plan? The answer is, you can't. You'll probably have to write this section later if you plan to use it. I'm merely pointing out where the purpose belongs in the overall structure of the plan.

TABLE OF CONTENTS.

I. THE BUSINESS

A. *Business Description*

1. Name. This is usually a one-liner such as: "The name of this business is Imports Plus Incorporated." Be certain, if the business is a corporation, to use the terms Incorporated (or Inc.) or Corporation (Corp.)
2. Location. Again, this is usually simple: "The business is located at 3200 Front Street, Elkhart, Indiana."
3. Physical Facilities. Example: "Imports Plus, Inc., leases 5,000 square feet of retail space at sidewalk level. Approximately 3,500 square feet are devoted to counters and shelves to display goods. The remaining 1,500 square feet contain a storeroom and an office."

B. *Products or Services*

1. Description of Product Line. In this section you must describe what you plan to sell in such a way that any reader will understand your intentions. Because most startups deal with what's called normal businesses (restaurant, clothing store, machine shop, income tax service), these descriptions don't have to be too detailed. However, if you're starting a unique variation of a common business (a shop selling only women's sleepwear, a word processing service bureau), more detail is necessary.
2. Proprietary Considerations. Most financing sources look for the USP—unique selling proposition—of a business, and every business has one.

   Example of USPs are
   >a manufactured product that is patented.
   >the unique personality of the owner.
   >a lifetime warranty.
   >an excellent location.
   >a name with great appeal.

   IBM's USP for its larger computers over the years has been not technical superiority (companies like Univac and Control Data Corporation were often judged to have "better" machines) nor price (IBM usually had the highest price), but its commitment to customer service. Give this paragraph some careful thought; it's very important. You can always discover your USP if you look carefully enough.

C. *Management Plan*

1. Organizational Form and Structure. If the business is a sole proprietorship and you're the proprietor with no employees, say so. If the business is a partnership, name those partners and designate their legal relationship (general or limited) as well as their financial relationship (amount of investment, percent of profits). If a corporation, give the name of the state and the date of incorporation. There are cases in which a business is not yet formed because the entrepreneur wants to see which form investors prefer—limited partnership or stockholder—but this isn't common. Also, if your business is going to start with a few employees, draw an organization chart showing who does what and to whom they report.
2. Resumés of Key People. Usually this is just yourself. Make the resumé easy to read, more like a biography than the terse style

used for job applications. Stress accomplishments and be sure to point out any past experience in the kind of business you're opening. Stick to facts and don't ramble.

3. Staffing Plan. This section only applies if you plan significant growth in the next three years. Think through how many people you'll need, when, how much you'll pay them, and the skills you want them to have.

4. Supporting Services. Names of individuals, their firms, and addresses. Scratch out any that don't apply.

D. *Operations Plan*

1. Facilities and Equipment. If you need to expand I., A., 3., Physical Facilities, do it here. If you're starting a small manufacturing company, draw a floor plan. If you're going to need equipment (lathes, computer, deep-fat fryers), list what you'll need.

2. Plans For Growth and Expansion. Many entrepreneurs start quite small, even when they operate the business on a full-time basis, and grow as time and capital permit. A small lunch counter may eventually become a full restaurant. A retail business such as a hardware store may evolve into a home center. If you plan to grow in the first three years, specify how this expansion will take place. Will you add more space? More products or services? Remember, physical growth—more space, more products, more sales—must be balanced by the staffing plan (I., C., 3) and your financial projections (Section III).

3. Overall Schedule. In the last chapter you completed a schedule of the activities leading up to starting the business. Now look forward three years into the operation of the business. You have some choices here. Many times it makes sense to combine this schedule with the previous section on growth and expansion. You can also do this part as a separate section, using the same graphic approach as the timing exercise in Chapter Three, or simply listing the events and approximately when they will occur.

4. Process Description. This section is normally used only for a manufacturing business; it allows the entrepreneur to describe the process by which goods will be produced. If you're beginning such a venture, it's important to tell the reader how your operation works. Sometimes a floor plan of the manufacturing (production) process, showing the flow of material and the individual operations, is included. If your business is something other than manufacturing, you can probably ignore this section unless you plan to operate in a manner quite different from your competition.

E. *Risks* (optional)

There is controversy about whether a section on the risks of a particular startup should be included in a business plan. Some authorities suggest that pointing out pitfalls weakens a business plan by bringing up negative factors. Others say it represents total honesty on the part of the entrepreneur. If you're seeking equity funds, address the risks of the venture, if for no other reason than the legalities of raising money by selling stock in a non-existent business. When doing this, you come under "blue sky" laws, the basic intent of which is to protect an investor from being hoodwinked. If you accept equity money, don't fully inform the investor of the nature of his or her investment, and the enterprise fails, that investor may sue for his or her money. If you specify the risks in the prospectus, you usually absolve yourself from liability.

Only discuss unique and significant risks. Don't bring up such things as the possibility of fire or theft or storms; those are normal risks which all businesses face. Items that may be listed are:

1. Selling to one small market segment.
2. Obtaining goods from a single supplier.
3. Being the first with the business idea.
4. Entering a technological field more easily served by a large corporation.
5. Getting into a business dependent on rapid change in customer buying habits (high fashion, for example).

If you're selling stock, that is, offering securities, be certain to get legal help because, often, official wording must be used. Some prospectuses I've seen contain the following clause, often in capital letters or even red ink:

THIS IS A HIGH RISK VENTURE.
NO ONE SHOULD PURCHASE SHARES OF STOCK
IN THIS CORPORATION WHO IS NOT PREPARED
TO LOSE ALL OR A SIGNIFICANT PORTION OF
THAT INVESTMENT.

Strong language, indeed, but sometimes necessary.

II. MARKETING PLAN

A. Marketing Research

1. Description of the Market. This section and the one which follows, Industry Trends, are often combined into one. If you decide to separate the two, describe in this section the market for your goods and services in terms of:
   a. the size of the market in annual sales, both nationally and locally;
   b. what characterizes that market: long-standing versus a new market (steel versus home computers, for example); how and why customers buy, and the number of competitors; the ease of entry into the market (service is generally easy, manufacturing difficult); special qualifications required by business owners (knowledge of accounting for a bookkeeping service); special problems and opportunities.
2. Industry Trends. I strongly suggest that you consult periodicals as well as the Department of Commerce's U.S. Industrial Outlook; then discuss:
   a. a brief history of the market as a whole, its changes and growth rates.
   b. projections and forecasts for the market. For example, I did a study for a new restaurant and found the percentage of the food dollar spent on eating out was forecast to increase about 0.4 percent per year.
   c. factors relating to growth (or decline). In the above example, one reason for the increase was the tendency for more people in a household to work.
   d. the sensitivity of the market to external factors such as the state of the economy. The sale of beer increases in tough times, for instance.
   e. local factors affecting your sales if your market is not national.
3. Target Market. Every small and most large businesses have a target market. Target your own market carefully so you can relate to the needs of those potential customers. If yours is a con-

sumer market, categorize your customers by geography, age, sex, income level, ethnic group. You may also describe how and what this group buys relative to your business—a male teenager purchases more fad items with his allowance than a retired person with established wealth. Your market could be institutional—large businesses, machine shops in New Jersey, all hospitals, the Federal Government. Numbers are important. When I was in my medical electronics business, one of our target markets was physicians in general practice. At the time there were 746,000 of them in the United States alone. Based on surveys we had calculated, we could sell a $300 instrument to one-quarter of one percent of the g.p.'s per year. Thus our annual sales would be

$$746,000 \times 0.0025 \times \$300 = \$559,500$$

This section is also the proper place to discuss the results of the marketing research outlined in the previous chapter.

4. Competition. If you did your homework in Chapter Three, this section is a piece of cake. Take a minimum of three competitors and discuss their strengths and weaknesses as you see them.

B. *Objectives and Strategy*

A simpler way to describe this section is: "What I'm going to do and how I'm going to do it." Again, the time period is three years, with detailed attention given to the first year. Too many entrepreneurs simply "open up" with little or no thought about how they're going to secure customers. Naturally, your objectives (goals) and the various strategies to reach them come from your marketing research. The more you know about your customers, their needs, and the competition's strong and weak points, the better the position you're in to plan your moves.

There's no established format for this section; it can be done in prose form or it can be done as a table:

Objective	Strategy
Attain early income levels as shown in financial projections.	Open business with a sale to be announced in advance on radio and in local papers. Conduct sale for two weeks.
Increase profit from 5 percent to 7 percent after first six months	Raise prices 11 percent; inform customers one month in advance.
Secure 20 distributors in first six months.	Conduct mail campaign to potential distributors, using a mailing list.
Begin sales to U.S. Government by second year.	Get on bidders' lists during first year.
Build mailing list	Buy ad in "Yankee" magazine for 12 months.

The more specific you are with strategies and objectives, the more measurable your results will be.

C. *Pricing Policy*

Most entrepreneurs set their prices by one or more of three different ways:

1. By calculation: markup, gross margin, or return on investment.
2. As a result of the environment: competition, convention, government regulations.
3. As a marketing strategy: a very high price for a unique product (called skim-the-cream pricing), a very low price to gain market share (called penetration pricing), sale pricing.

Discuss how you plan to set your prices. It may be simple—100 percent markup on cost—or quite complex—beginning with high prices and successively lowering them as competition enters the market. Remember your marketing research and what it told you about pricing and customer response.

D. *Sales Terms*

This is usually pretty simple, and for many small businesses the terms are "cash and carry." In addition, you may use bank credit cards (VISA, MasterCard), other cards (American Express, Diner's Club), or grant trade credit. If the latter is the case, specify payment terms: net 30; 2 percent–10 days, net 30; and so on.

E. *Method of Sales and Distribution*

In most small business startups, the selling is done by the entrepreneur and there is no distribution. This might change in the second or third year, though. There are other forms of sales and distribution that can be used for more complex businesses. For example, the business may do its own distributing to its end customers and use sales clerks on premises, its own sales force calling on customers, or independent sales representatives taking orders. Another form of internal distribution is mail order. External distribution means sales to an intermediary such as a distributor or a dealer.

F. *Customer Service*

This may be non-existent for your business. This doesn't mean that you don't heed the concerns of your customers; customer service refers, for instance, to a returns policy, money-back guarantees, or fulfillment of warranties. If you're going to sell appliances, for example, you may want to offer a repair service.

G. *Advertising and Promotion*

What you must address here is:

1. Your means of communicating with your potential customers: newspaper, radio, magazines, direct mail, telephone.
2. The role of your ad agency if you're using one.
3. A timetable of media usage (radio and newspaper ads, each on a daily basis for the first six months), the scope of usage (4-inch by 4-column, 30-second spot), and its cost.
4. The basic message that you're communicating, especially if you're using image advertising rather than specific products or services advertising.
5. Any promotion you have: opening day ceremony, press releases, appearance of some reknowned person at your place of business, a balloon race that you sponsor.

H. *Forecasts*

In this section show your forecasts for business for the first three years. If you deal with one or just a few products, show the forecast by both units and dollars. Suppose you're going to sell two brands of small computers, one at $200 and the second at $600. Your sales forecast might look like this:

	Model A Units	($200) Dollars	Model B Units	($600) Dollars	Annual Sales In Total
Year 1	600	$120,000	100	$ 60,000	$180,000
Year 2	850	170,000	180	108,000	278,000
Year 3	1,000	200,000	225	135,000	335,000

If your business sells many products, simply show the total annual sales. Remember, these forecasts must come from *somewhere:* your marketing research. If they have thought and reason behind them, you can explain to a bank or an investor how the numbers were developed.

Also, the forecasts become one of the important factors for the entire section to follow—the financial section.

III. FINANCIAL DATA

Before beginning these sections, please note we'll be using terms from accounting and finance—proforma profit and loss, balance sheet, breakeven analysis. Because I'll give brief explanations but won't go into detail, I strongly suggest you spend the necessary time becoming totally familiar with these terms. To do this you can:

1. Take a basic accounting course at your nearest college or vocational-technical school.
2. Spend time in the library reading books on small business finance. I like *Simplified Accounting For Non-Accountants* by Hayes and Baker (Wiley, 1980).
3. Obtain the materials mentioned before (*Small-Time Operator, Business Planning Guide*) as well as these free or very inexpensive publications:
   a. "How to Read a Financial Report," available free from Merrill, Lynch, Pierce, Fenner & Smith, Inc., 165 Broadway, New York, NY 10080.
      It's excellent.
   b. A free listing of currently available reports is available from Small Business Reporter, Bank of America, Box 37000, San Francisco, CA 94137.
      These reports cost less than $5.00 each, and although they change their offerings from time to time they are quite helpful. Some recent report topics include:

      "Financing Small Business"
      "Steps to Starting a Business"
      "Understanding Financial Statements"
      "Cash Flow/Cash Management"

   c. Visit your nearest SBA office (see Appendix A) and ask for their free business startup package. Be certain to obtain the brochure on the business plan for your kind of business. Currently, there are four brochures available—retailers, service firms, construction firms, and manufacturers.
4. Have your accountant or a qualified business consultant explain terms and/or help you with any parts you don't understand.

Ready? Let's go.

A. *Proposal*

If you wrote a "Purpose" paragraph in the beginning of the plan, there's no need to repeat it here. If you didn't, state what funds you want to raise. See page 46 for examples. Remember, you have to complete the financial projections before doing this section. This holds for the next section as well; I'm showing where these items belong physically. Business plan readers like to see summaries *before* they get to the detailed stuff.

B. *Use of Proceeds*

This is most often done in tabular form. For example:

Sources of Funds

Owner's equity	$20,000
Other equity	15,000
Bank loan	30,000
	$65,000

Use of Proceeds

Cash on hand	$ 5,000
Inventory	26,000
Legal and Accounting Fees	2,000
Advertising	3,000
Cash register	2,000
Shelves and displays	6,000
Deposits (utility, telephone)	500
Leasehold improvements	19,000
Two months' rent	1,500
	$65,000

This allows investors and especially the bank to know where the money's going.

C. *Opening Day Balance Sheet*

Here's where you may need some help. It's not hard to do a balance sheet, especially one for your opening day, because you'll probably only have a few assets (cash, inventory, leasehold improvements, equipment) and a few liabilities (some accounts payable such as inventory, legal fees, advertising bill, a bank loan). The owner's equity item shows the amount of money you and any investor have put in. Remember, assets must equal liabilities *plus* owner's equity. It all works like the net worth statement you did in Chapter Three.

D. *Cash Flow Projections*

This is the big one, the one we've all been waiting for. Because the cash flow projection is so important, I'm going to have you do a little more work here. I want you to plan your finances very carefully in a way that allows you to figure out how much money you need.

First, you need to figure your startup costs.

These are expenses occurring before opening day. There's a blank form (borrowed from the SBA's recommendation) on page 24 in the business plan workbook for your use. Please do it in pencil.

I'm going to do an example along with you to give an idea of

STARTUP COSTS

Name of Business: The Darning Needle

1. Real estate, furniture, fixtures, machinery, equipment
   a. Purchase price (if paid in full with cash) $ —
   b. Down payment (if paid on contract) 770
   c. Transportation/installation costs 130
2. Starting inventory 16,000
3. Decorating and remodeling 1,500
4. Deposits
   a. Utilities, Telephone 500
   b. Rents 600
   c. Other (specify): —
5. Fees
   a. Professional (legal, accounting) 1,300
   b. Licenses, permits, taxes 200
   c. Other (specify): Society membership 100
6. Advertising (initial) 1,200
7. Salaries/owner's draw until business opens 500
8. Other: stationery and forms 600

TOTAL STARTUP COSTS $23,400

how this is all done. We'll begin with the startup cost form prepared by the owner of a fabric shop, The Darning Needle. I have chosen a retail establishment for this example because the plan is simpler than a manufacturing plan yet more complex than that for most service businesses. Again, refer to Appendix C for a simple plan for manufacturing. I'm not going to go through a line-by-line explanation of every item on the form (you should know what these mean by now), but I do want to talk about item 2, the starting inventory. Many entrepreneurs want to know how much inventory to start with. Here's one way to figure it for a drugstore.

First consult Robert Morris' *Annual Statement Studies* and find drug stores by SIC code and the ratio called cost of sales/inventory (this is also called inventory turnover or cost of sales percentage). If we discover from our marketing research that the first-year estimated sales for a drugstore are $300,000, then we can figure opening inventory as follows:

Using the Robert Morris data for a drugstore (SIC 5912)

cost of sales: 65%
cost of sales/inventory: 4.0 times per year

and our estimated first year's sales, we can determine how much our total annual inventory will cost:

$$0.65 \times \$300,000 = \$195,000$$

Because this represents a "turnover" of four times, your initial inventory is:

$$\frac{\$195,000}{4} = \$48,750$$

$48,750, then, is a good estimate to begin with. If you can't find your type of business in the Robert Morris guide, you can do one or more of the following:

... call your banker, accountant, or SBA representative.

... spend some time in a library.

... visit businesses similar to yours and estimate how much inventory they have on hand.

... calculate an inventory level of, say, two months. If you use two months, your turnover is six times per year, so you would multiply your annual sales estimate by the percentage of costs of sales, then divide by six.

Taking our estimated $23,400 startup costs, (page 54) let's move to the monthly cash flow projection (preliminary) using the first of the blank financial forms on page 24a of the workbook.

Why is this form called preliminary? For two reasons. (1) it's a worksheet on which you'll probably make a number of changes (use pencil please) and (2) we're going to use it to figure out how much outside funding is required.

For our example, we need to know how much money our entrepreneur has as an initial investment. This figure is most often derived from the personal net worth statement—how many assets will be turned into cash.

Let's say our entrepreneur, Leslie O'Keefe, has $27,700 as her initial investment. She's going to open the doors of her fabric, yarn, and pattern shop called The Darning Needle on August 1st. Today is June 16th. She fills in the headings on the preliminary cash flow projection and designates the 12 months over which the projection will be done.

Leslie begins with August and shows her initial investment ($27,-700) and her startup costs of $23,400 which occur before August 1st. On opening day she has beginning cash of $4,300; this is what's left from the original investment after paying for inventory, remodeling, and the like.

Next she estimates her cash sales for August—$5,000—and any accounts receivable collected—none for the first month. You see that item 7 is for loans and other cash made available to the business—equity investment, sale of assets, tax rebates, return of security deposits. Item 7 is left blank on the preliminary form. We'll return to it later.

She figures her total available cash for August ($9,300), the sum of beginning cash ($4,300) and cash sales ($5,000). Now she estimates her expenses. Let me very briefly define expense items, numbers 11 through 30.

11. Purchase of inventory. This is merchandise for resale, in the case of retail, or for conversion, in the case of manufacturing. Note that Leslie shows no expense for August because she already spent $16,000 before August—see her startup costs.

12. Employee wages. Base pay less taxes (including FICA). Notice that she plans to bring a sales clerk aboard in November.

13. Payroll taxes and expense. This includes federal withholding, FICA (employee's and employer's portions), unemployment insurance, and benefits—health insurance, pension. This value can be 15 to 50 percent of item 12, plus item 30.

14. Outside services. Subcontracted work, janitorial service, trash or scrap pickup, snow removal. Do not include accounting or legal expenses.

15. Business supplies. Office supplies (paper, forms, file folders) and operating supplies (cleaning agents, lubricants, chemicals).

16. Repairs and maintenance. This has more relevance for manu-

MONTHLY CASH FLOW PROJECTION (Preliminary Worksheet)

Name of Business: The Darning Needle   Address: Front Street,

		Year: 19XX – 19X1 Month	1 Aug.	2 Sept.	3 Oct.	4 Nov.	5 Dec.
1		Your investment	27700				
2	Less:	Startup costs	23400				
3							
4		Beginning cash	4300	100	(3530)	(6780)	(9990)
5	Plus:	Cash sales	5000	7000	7000	10000	17500
6		Collection of A/R	—	200	600	800	1000
7		Loans, other (specify)					
8							
9	Total available cash		9300	7300	4070	4020	8510
10	Expenses						
11		Purchase of inventory	—	2760	3500	4800	6200
12		Employee wages	—	—	—	1000	1800
13		Payroll taxes & exp.	260	260	260	520	750
14		Outside services	80	80	80	80	80
15		Business suplies	1700	400	200	300	400
16		Repairs and maint.	—	100	—	—	100
17		Advertising	1400	1600	1600	2600	1200
18		Car, delivery, travel	500	600	600	400	500
19		Acctg. & legal	400	300	200	200	200
20		Rent	1200	1200	1200	1200	1200
21		Telephone	420	480	350	300	400
22		Utilities	200	260	290	340	400
23		Insurance	370	—	—	200	
24		Taxes	—	120	—	—	—
25		Equipment	770	770	770	770	770
26		Other					
27		Postage & Printing	400	400	300	400	500
28		Loan repayment					
29		Miscellaneous	500	500	500	500	500
30		Owner's withdrawal	1000	1000	1000	1000	1200
31	Total expenses		9200	10830	10850	14010	16200
32	Ending cash (9 less 31)		100	(3530)	(6780)	(9990)	(7690)
33							
34							
35							

Anytown   Prepared by: Leslie O'Keefe   Date: June 16, 19XX

	Jan.	Feb.	Mar.	Apr.	May	June	Jul	Total 12 Months	
	6	7	8	9	10	11	12	13	
1									
2									
3									
4	(7690)	(6490)	(6890)	(7640)	(3990)	(310)	3250		
5	12000	13200	14700	18500	18900	22000	20000	165800	
6	1800	1400	1000	1000	1700	2000	2400	13900	
7									
8									
9	6110	8110	8810	11860	16610	23690	25650	179700	
10									
11	5000	6900	7400	7700	8400	11400	12800	76860	
12	1000	1000	1000	1000	1100	1100	1100	10100	
13	600	600	600	600	700	800	800	6750	
14	80	80	80	80	80	80	80	960	
15	200	200	300	200	200	200	300	4600	
16	-	-	100	-	-	-	100	400	
17	600	1000	1200	1200	1300	1300	1500	15900	
18	300	300	350	350	350	350	350	4950	
19	200	200	300	200	200	260	400	3060	
20	1200	1200	1200	1200	1200	1200	1200	14400	
21	300	300	300	300	300	300	360	4110	
22	450	450	340	250	220	100	100	3400	
23	-	-	510	-	-	200	-	1280	
24	100	-	-	-	-	180	-	400	
25	770	770	770	770	770	770	770	9240	
26									
27	100	300	300	300	400	400	400	4200	
28									
29	500	500	500	500	500	500	500	6000	
30	1200	1200	1200	1200	1200	1300	1300	13800	
31	12600	15000	16450	15850	16920	20440	22060	180410	
32	(6490)	(6890)	(7640)	(3990)	(310)	3250	3590	(710)	
33									
34									
35									

facturing than for retail or service. It should also include fixing-up and decorating costs like painting.

17. Advertising. Include Yellow Pages cost. Notice that Leslie increases advertising as Christmas approaches.
18. Car, delivery, travel. Some businesses will lease or purchase a vehicle for delivery. Also any travel and entertainment expense belongs here.
19. Accounting and legal. Self-explanatory.
20. Rent. Please note that this is for real estate only. It does not include equipment rental; see item 25 for this.
21. Telephone. Self-explanatory.
22. Utilities. Heat, electricity, water.
23. Insurance. All business insurance: key person, liability, contents, workmen's compensation.
24. Taxes. Real estate taxes, inventory taxes, sales taxes, franchise fee.
25. Equipment. This is used for either outright purchases or for rental on such items as cash registers, machine tools, postal meters, copiers, typewriters, computers.
26–27. Other. Note that Leslie has added a category for postage and printing.
28. Loan repayment. Left blank for now.
29. Miscellaneous. Small accounts including petty cash for which separate categories are not practical.
30. Owner's withdrawal. Leslie is going to take out $1,000 a month until December when she gives herself a raise.

When Leslie completes her expenses for August, she totals them in item 31 and substracts the total expenses from the total available cash (item 9). This subtraction produces item 32, the ending cash for August which is also the beginning cash for September.

The process of estimation continues month by month until one year is completed. Notice that the ending cash item reaches its maximum deficit (denoted by the parentheses) in November at $9,990. That's how much *more* money Leslie is going to need to operate her business. Let's assume she wants to borrow all she needs; should she borrow exactly $9,990? No, for three reasons. In the first place, when she adds her loan payment back in, as she does in her next cash flow projection, that makes the deficit larger. Secondly, she allows a risk factor of 10 to 20 percent because sales may not be as high as expected, expenses may be greater, or both. Thirdly, she doesn't want the cash account to go to zero, but rather wants some reserve.

She rounds the $9,990 to an even $10,000 and adds 10 percent for safety to make it $11,000. Finally, because she wants a minimum cash level in the business of $4,000, she makes a loan request of $15,000.

How does she figure her monthly payment? She calls the bank, which gives her different figures for the different kinds of loans available. One interest rate and length of loan is for real estate, another for inventory, a third for equipment. The table on the next page shows how interest rate and loan length affect payments. In our example, Leslie assumes her $15,000 loan will be at 14 percent for eight years giving her a monthly payment of

$$15 \times \$17.37 = \$260.55$$

Now she goes to the next projection (pages 60 and 61) and adds in the loan proceeds of $15,000, occurring in August, and the payment of $260 each month under item 28.

Before we go on, I want to point out that the preliminary projection must balance, and there's an easy way to check this. Notice the very last entry (item 32 July), the ending cash $3,590. That figure is obtained by subtracting the total annual expenses of $180,-410 from the total annual sales of $179,700 producing a deficit of $710. That $710 must represent the overall reduction in cash throughout the year and it does. We started with $4,300 (item 4, August) in cash and ended with $3,590, a $710 reduction.

The final projection is a piece of cake. The $15,000 loan is put in the first month (item 7, August) and each month shows a payment, principal and interest, of $260. The cash calculations are conducted as before. To prove the overall method, Leslie substracts beginning cash in August (item 4), $4,300, from ending cash in July, $15,470 (item 32), giving $11,170, the difference between cash in and cash out (item 32) in the 12-month summary.

MONTHLY PAYMENTS ON $1,000								
Interest Rate	**6%**	**8%**	**10%**	**12%**	**14%**	**16%**	**18%**	**20%**
Years								
5	19.33	20.28	21.25	22.24	23.27	24.32	25.39	26.49
6	16.57	17.53	18.53	19.55	20.61	21.69	22.81	23.95
7	14.61	15.59	16.60	17.65	18.74	19.86	21.02	22.21
8	13.14	14.14	15.17	16.25	17.37	18.53	19.72	20.95
9	12.01	13.02	14.08	15.18	16.33	17.53	18.76	20.03
10	11.10	12.13	13.22	14.35	15.53	16.75	18.02	19.33
11	10.37	11.42	12.52	13.68	14.89	16.14	17.44	18.79
12	9.76	10.82	11.95	13.13	14.37	15.66	16.99	18.37
13	9.25	10.33	11.48	12.69	13.95	15.27	16.63	18.04
14	8.81	9.91	11.08	12.31	13.60	14.95	16.34	17.77
15	8.44	9.56	10.75	12.00	13.32	14.69	16.10	17.56

Notes: 1. For intermediate interest rates, use half the difference.
     Example: 11% for 8 Years
       12% rate: $16.25
       10% rate: -15.17
               $\$1.08 \div 2 = \$0.54 + \$15.17 = \$15.71$

    2. Multiply loan in thousands of dollars to get actual payment.
       Example: Loan of $27,500 for 10 years at 14%.
       Table gives $15.53 for $1,000 loan.
       Payment: $27.5 \times \$15.53 = \$427.08$

Notice that Leslie's cash balance reaches a minimum of $3,970 in November, pretty close to the $4,000 minimum she wants.

Doing cash flow projections beyond the first year is optional but recommended. Many entrepreneurs do the second and third years by quarters, using a form like the one in the workbook.

Well, if you've made it this far, most of the work has been done. The next sections of the business plan are also optional but recommended. They take some effort but nothing like the cash flow projections.

E. *Pro Forma Income Statements*

An income statement differs from a cash flow projection in that it's prepared for accounting and tax purposes. Pro forma simply means in the future. We're not going to go into preparation in detail, but I want you to be aware of two major differences between income and cash flow statements.

MONTHLY CASH FLOW PROJECTION

Name of Business: **The Darning Needle**   Address: **Front Street,**

		Year: 19XX – 19X1	1 Aug	2 Sep	3 Oct	4 Nov	5 Dec
1		Your investment	27700				
2	Less:	Startup costs	23400				
3							
4		Beginning cash	4300	14840	10950	7440	3970
5	Plus:	Cash sales	5000	7000	7000	10000	17500
6		Collection of A/R	—	200	600	800	1000
7		Loans, other (specify)	15000	—	—	—	—
8							
9		Total available cash	24300	22040	18550	18240	22470
10	**Expenses**						
11		Purchase of inventory	—	2760	3500	4800	6200
12		Employee wages	—	—	—	1000	1800
13		Payroll taxes & exp.	260	260	260	520	750
14		Outside services	80	80	80	80	80
15		Business suplies	1700	400	200	300	400
16		Repairs and maint.	—	100	—	—	100
17		Advertising	1400	1600	1600	2000	1200
18		Car, delivery, travel	500	600	600	400	500
19		Acctg. & legal	400	300	200	200	200
20		Rent	1200	1200	1200	1200	1200
21		Telephone	420	480	350	300	400
22		Utilities	200	260	290	340	400
23		Insurance	370	—	—	200	—
24		Taxes	—	120	—	—	—
25		Equipment	770	770	770	770	770
26		Other					
27		Postage & Printing	400	400	300	400	500
28		Loan repayment	260	260	260	260	260
29		Miscellaneous	500	500	500	500	500
30		Owner's withdrawal	1000	1000	1000	1000	1200
31	**Total expenses**		9460	11090	11110	14270	16460
32	**Ending cash (9 less 31)**		14840	10950	7440	3970	6010
33							
34							
35							

Anytown   Prepared by: *Leslie O'Keefe*   Date: June 16, 19XX

	Jan	Feb	Mar	Apr	May	Jun	Jul	Total 12 Months	
	6	7	8	9	10	11	12	13	
1	╳	╳	╳	╳	╳	╳	╳		1
2									2
3									3
4	6010	6950	6290	5280	8670	12090	15390		4
5	12000	13200	14700	18500	18900	22000	20000	165800	5
6	1800	1400	1000	1000	1700	2000	2400	13900	6
7	—	—	—	—	—	—	—	15000	7
8									8
9	19810	21550	21990	24780	29270	36090	37790	194700	9
10									10
11	5000	6900	7400	7700	8400	11400	12800	76860	11
12	1000	1000	1000	1000	1100	1100	1100	10100	12
13	600	600	600	600	700	800	800	6750	13
14	80	80	80	80	80	80	80	960	14
15	200	200	300	200	200	200	300	4600	15
16	-	—	100	—	—	—	100	400	16
17	600	1000	1200	1200	1300	1300	1500	15900	17
18	300	300	350	350	350	350	350	4950	18
19	200	200	300	200	200	260	400	3060	19
20	1200	1200	1200	1200	1200	1200	1200	14400	20
21	300	300	300	300	300	300	360	4100	21
22	450	450	340	250	220	100	100	3400	22
23	—	—	510	—	—	200	—	1280	23
24	100	—	—	—	—	180	—	400	24
25	770	770	770	770	770	770	770	9240	25
26									26
27	100	300	300	300	400	400	400	4200	27
28	260	260	260	260	260	260	260	3120	28
29	500	500	500	500	500	500	500	6000	29
30	1200	1200	1200	1200	1200	1200	1300	13800	30
31	12860	15260	16770	16110	17180	20700	22320	183530	31
32	6950	6290	5280	8670	12090	15390	15470	11170	32
33									33
34									34
35									35

1. An income statement doesn't show the total loan payment—it shows the interest portion of the loan, because only that part is a deductible expense for tax purposes.
2. If you purchase a fixed asset—vehicle, computer, display case— you can't deduct the full cost of that asset; you can only *depreciate* a portion of it and you must do that according to changeable IRS guidelines.

Below is an approximation of an income statement for The Darning Needle using figures from the 12-month total of the cash flow projection (pages 60 and 61) plus startup costs (page 54). Although it's not exactly correct*, it gives the basic idea. The blank form is on workbook page 26 and may be copied if you wish to do more than one year's.

PRO FORMA INCOME STATEMENT
THE DARNING NEEDLE

for the business year August 19xx to July 19xx

			Percent
Net Sales		$179,700	100.0
Cost of Goods Sold		76,860	42.8
Gross Margin		$102,840	57.2
Expenses			
Payroll expense	$31,150		17.3
Outside services	960		0.5
Business supplies	4,600		2.6
Repairs and maintenance	400		0.2
Advertising	7,100		4.0
Car, delivery, travel	4,950		2.8
Accounting and legal	4,360		2.4
Rent	15,000		8.3
Telephone and utilities	8,010		4.5
Insurance	1,280		0.7
Taxes	600		0.3
Equipment rental	10,140		5.6
Depreciation	320		0.2
Postage and printing	4,800		2.7
Interest	2,030		1.1
Miscellaneous	6,100		3.4
Total Expenses		101,800	56.6
Profit (Loss) before tax		$ 1,040	0.6
Federal and state tax (20%)		210	0.1
Profit after tax		$ 830	0.5

Let me briefly describe how I obtained the figures for the pro forma income statement:

Net Sales. The cash sales (item 5, $165,800) plus collected receivables (item 6, $13,900) gives a total of $179,700. Because I show all other entries as a percent of sales, the $179,700 is shown as 100.0 percent.

---

* There are several reasons for this. One is that the sales figure should be higher because of sales on credit. Accountants will tell you there's been a *sale* even though the money hasn't been collected.

Cost of Goods Sold. I use the amount of inventory purchases for the year (item 11, $76,860). This isn't totally correct because I should start with beginning inventory, add in the purchases for the year, and subtract the ending inventory. It's close enough for our purposes though.

Gross Margin. Net Sales minus Cost of Goods Sold.

Payroll Expense. Consists of

Owner's draw before opening	$ 500
Owner's annual draw	13,800
Employee wages	10,100
Payroll taxes and expenses	6,750
	$31,150

Outside Services. Same as cash flow.

Business Supplies. Same as cash flow.

Repairs and Maintenance. Same as cash flow.

Advertising

Initial	$ 1,200
For the year	5,900
	$ 7,100

Car, delivery, travel. Same as cash flow.

Accounting and legal

Initial	$ 1,300
For the year	3,060
	$ 4,360

Rent

Rent deposit	$ 600
Annual rent	14,400
	$15,000

Telephone & Utilities

Deposits	$ 500
Telephone	4,110
Utilities	3,400
	$ 8,010

Insurance. Same as cash flow.

Taxes

Initial	$ 200
Annual	400
	$ 600

Equipment rental

Down payment	$ 770
Installation	130
Annual	9,240
	$10,140

Depreciation. Your accountant can give you these values.
21 percent of the $1,500 remodeling charge: $315 rounded to $320.

Postage and Printing

Initial	$ 600
Annual	4,200
	$ 4,800

Interest

During the first twelve months, total payments on Leslie's $15,000 loan (14 percent for 8 years) are $3,126.60. Of that, $2,031.50 is interest and $1,095.10 is principal, reducing the loan balance to $13,904.90. You need a fancy calculator to determine this, or your banker or accountant can help you.

Miscellaneous

Society membership	$ 100
Annual	6,000
	$6,100

Total Expenses. Self-explanatory

Profit (Loss) before tax. Gross margin less Total Expenses.

Federal and State tax. Rate is estimated at 20 percent.

Profit after tax. Self-explanatory.

F. Breakeven Analysis

This is a rather simple calculation used to find the breakeven point for a business, that *theoretical* amount of dollar sales at which the business neither makes nor loses money.

Many startups lose money in their first year; some actually continue losing money into the second and possibly even the third year. There's nothing wrong with this as long as the plan shows (1) why there are losses, and (2) that there is a definite intent to make a profit eventually. For example, a high-technology manufacturing startup like a computer company may lose money for five years because incoming sales revenue can't keep pace with planned growth. You can calculate the breakeven point in dollars of annual sales as follows:

$$\text{Breakeven} = \frac{\text{Fixed Costs (dollars annually)}}{\% \text{ Gross Margin (expressed as a decimal)}}$$

What are "fixed costs"? They are items such as rent that you pay whether or not you do any business. The simplest way to assess fixed costs is to use the total expenses from the income statement. This isn't exactly correct because there are variable expenses such as advertising which are not fixed the way rent, interest or insurance are, but the method is accurate enough. Let's look at a summary income statement:

		Percent
Net Sales	$200,000	100
Cost of Goods Sold	120,000	60
Gross Margin	$ 80,000	40
Expenses	100,000	(50)
Profit (Loss)	($ 20,000)	(10)

A banker or investor might want to know the breakeven point for this business, and it's *not* $220,000 ($200,000 sales plus the $20,000 loss). Using our formula

$$\text{Breakeven} = \frac{\$100,000}{0.40} = \$250,000$$

and we can prove this as follows:

		Percent
Net Sales	$250,000	100
Cost of Goods Sold	150,000	60
Gross Margin	$100,000	40
Expenses	100,000	40
Profit (Loss)	$ 0	0

You can see what happens: Sales rise to $250,000 and cost of goods sold stays at 60 percent of sales which brings it to $150,000. The expenses stay fixed at the same *dollar* amount of $100,000, which is 40 percent of sales. All this makes the profit zero: the new business has broken even.

The space below is for you to figure the breakeven point for The Darning Needle. HINT: Go to the pro forma income statement.

$$\text{Breakeven} = \frac{\$}{0.} = \quad \$$$

IV. APPENDICES

This is not a place to throw a lot of extraneous material just to make the plan/prospectus look fat. Use it only for items that don't fit else-where:

> . . . letters of intent from prospective customers.
> . . . government contracts.
> . . . photo of location.
> . . . architect's plan.
> . . . articles about the business.
> . . . advertising materials.

Summary

If you've come along through all this explanation and now have the rough draft of your plan, you've done a magnificent job. Only about one entrepreneur in fifteen is doing what you've done. Congratulations! I will once more remind you of the business plan for a manufacturing company in the Appendix.

So, you think you're ready to get your seed money now? Nope, not quite. There's still more preparation to do, but take heart. None of it is as tough as the business plan. What I want to do in the next chapter is talk about banks and bankers—what they look for, what they like and don't like. As one prominent banker told me, "If people do it *right,* we're suckers every time." I don't ever want you "suckering" a bank or anyone else; I just want you to have the advantage, and I want you to get your seed money and then run a successful enterprise.

Traditional Small Business Financing

The Entrepreneur

You must have *some* money if you want to start a business; that's what makes you an entrepreneur and not a promoter. Just how much money must you put into your business? Must you use every cent you have? Of course, this varies from person to person and situation to situation, but there are two things you'll hear from the financial community.

One, they want to see *some* commitment on your part. If you have $20,000 in a savings account or in stocks and bonds and are reluctant to put it into your new business, you'll have little success raising outside funds. People will wonder whether you have a personal stake in your business. Of course, you don't have to sell your furniture and appliances; but what about your house if you own one? Should you get a second mortage or pledge that asset as collateral on a loan? The answer is, in most cases, yes.

The second consideration is return on investment. If you're sure of yourself and your business idea, then the money you put into your business will be the best financial investment you can make. The harder you work to attain your business goals, the greater the return. Compare this to dumping $10,000 into the stock of some corporation; when the president of that company gets the flu or is found fooling around with his secretary, the price of the stock can plummet and you lose money through no fault of your own.

If you did your cash flow projection correctly, you know how much money you need from other sources. You may have been pleasantly surprised to discover you have enough dough to back the venture yourself. Or you may find that $5,000 from Aunt Sadie in addition to your funds will do it. But if you're like most folks, you're probably going to finance your startup with seed money from two places other than your own pocket: a commercial bank and a few friends and relatives. That is *traditional* small business financing. This chapter discusses those two approaches—acquaintances and bank—in detail.

Friends, Relatives, and Other Interested Parties

You approach private individuals because you don't have enough equity funds to *leverage* a bank loan. What do I mean by leverage? Let's look at an example.

If you buy a new car for $10,000, you have to put down money of your own. Let's say the bank wants 20 percent down, or $2,000. If you have the two grand, that's your *equity* investment. The bank then loans you the $8,000. If

66

you don't have the "downer," then you may have to go to Aunt Sadie to make up the difference.

Business works the same way. You need a downer before a bank will even talk to you. How much do you need? The answer depends on several factors—type of business, amount of collateral available, business conditions—but the range is 25 to 40 percent. Most bankers won't go for a deal where the debt-to-equity ratio is greater than 2:1. This means you need to have at least one-third ($33\frac{1}{3}$ percent) of the total funds in the form of equity.

Let's look at another example. Suppose the economy is a bit tight and your local commercial bank tells you they won't consider your deal unless the debt-to-equity ratio is 1.5:1 or less. Let's also assume you need $25,000 for your venture. Therefore

$$\frac{debt}{equity} = 1.5$$

and

$$debt + equity = \$25,000$$

By substituting, we see

$$
\begin{aligned}
1.5 \text{ equity} + \text{equity} &= \$25,000 \\
2.5 \text{ equity} &= \$25,000 \\
\text{equity} &= \frac{\$25,000}{2.5} = \$10,000
\end{aligned}
$$

and then because

$$
\begin{aligned}
debt &= \text{total needed} - \text{equity} \\
debt &= \$15,000
\end{aligned}
$$

To double-check

$$\frac{debt}{equity} = \frac{\$15,000}{\$10,000} = 1.5$$

Therefore, the bank will loan you $15,000 (60 percent of $25,000) of what you need if you come up with $10,000, or 40 percent. If you have $6,000 yourself, you need to raise the other four thousand from equity investments. Although you can get advice from your banker in advance, you should have your equity before you go to the bank for additional financing.

Besides friends and relatives as equity investors, talk to potential

   . . . business associates
   . . . employees
   . . . customers
   . . . suppliers

before you approach strangers.

Strangers willing to back you financially are usually men and women who are well off financially, and who are looking for a *sound* investment. The names of such potential investors may be learned from

   . . . your banker
   . . . your accountant and attorney
   . . . the local chamber of commerce
   . . . the local industrial development group

... an SBA representative
... your stockbroker
... your insurance agent.

You can also advertise in the newspaper but be certain to check with your lawyer for the correct wording. There are securities laws enacted to protect folks from scams; you won't run afoul of these if you follow your attorney's advice and explain to potential investors just what they're investing in. Your business plan/prospectus usually satisfies the legal requirements of "informing an investor."

We're going to discuss the corporate form of equity (buying stock) as opposed to the partnership form of equity (limited partners) because it's more common. However, remember what I said about holding the legal form of the business open if that's what your advisors suggest.

When you take in equity, you usually sell ownership in the corporation—shares of common stock. What happens when you sell common stock?

... You sell ownership.
... You provide your stockholder(s) with a stock certificate or other proof of ownership.
... You give your stockholder(s) voting privileges, usually one vote for each share of common stock.

How do you place a value on the stock of a business which, for all practical purposes, doesn't exist? You get the advice of your accountant and your attorney. What you're selling is an investment opportunity. Although dear Aunt Sadie wants to help you because you're her favorite niece, she should be shown what can happen to her investment if the business succeeds or fails.

Let's go back to our example in which you have $6,000 and need $4,000 in outside equity. Although you, as the founder of the business, could purchase your stock more cheaply—mainly because of the work that you do in putting the entire business together—let's say that Aunt Sadie is your outside stockholder and you each purchase stock at $1.00 per share. You then own 6,000 shares and your aunt 4,000. Because you have 60 percent of the votes and she has 40 percent, you have what is known as the controlling interest; i.e., you own more than 50 percent of the corporation. It is *generally* a good idea to maintain this control because if you don't you can be voted out.

How can we make this $4,000 a good investment for Aunt Sadie? Some people think they'll pay dividends on the stock, but that's extremely rare in small business. In the first place, the business needs every bit of cash it can use. Secondly, dividends come under what's known as double taxation; they're taxable to the corporation and the recipient as well. What you'll probably do is buy out Aunt Sadie when:

1. the business grows and has several profitable years;
2. the business can afford to do so either through the accumulation of a reserve fund or by borrowing.

Maybe in five years the value of Aunt Sadie's (and your) stock goes from $1.00 to $3.00 a share. If you and your aunt have the proper legal agreement, you pay her $12,000 for her 4,000 shares. She triples her money in five years. Not bad! When you buy her out, you then own 6,000 shares or 100 percent of the corporation. Aunt Sadie's stock returns to the corporation and becomes treasury stock, that which was once issued and is now repurchased. It sits in the *treasury* and can be re-issued without changing the by-laws.

If you can't buy out Aunt Sadie, she remains a stockholder until "something" happens. That something could be her death, in which case you might have to satisfy her heirs. Maybe they want cash and not some green certificate with naked people on it. Or, that something could be the sale of the business. In any case, you need legal assistance. Your lawyer may suggest restricted stock. Aunt Sadie might be a sweet person who doesn't understand business, but you don't want her selling her stock to some sharpie who's only going to be a lot of trouble to you. If you sell her restricted stock, she must sign an agreement not to sell her stock or at least to give you first right of refusal if she gets an offer to sell.

If you need to go beyond the Aunt Sadie's of the world, you'll wind up talking with individuals who are fairly knowledgeable about business. Here are some guidelines for you:

1. If you're asked a question and don't know the answer, say so. Don't fumble through. Tell the person you'll get the answer.
2. The really good investor certainly wants a return on his or her investment but usually understands risk.
3. More than the business idea, investors will be looking at you. Successful *people* run successful businesses.
4. If one or several of these potential investors seems to be something other than honest and forthright, back off.

You may want to hold an open meeting at the local Holiday Inn to present your business opportunity to a number of people at one time. There's nothing wrong with this; neither is there anything wrong with putting an ad in the paper to announce your meeting. If you do it this way, be sure you:

... don't make any outrageous claims such as saying this is the investment opportunity of a lifetime;
... have copies of the prospectus available for all;
... have your attorney, accountant, and banker at the meeting;
... make the presentation. Your advisors can help to clarify certain technical points, but it's *your* show;
... don't use any approach that looks like a Florida land sale;
... are honest. If you discuss opportunity, also discuss risk;
... have charts or other visual aids to help you make major points.

One other valuable consideration is the creation of an escrow account for stockholder investments. Your attorney will probably tell you it's not a good idea to start spending your stockholders' money before all the financing is in place. Because one reason you're using equity is to leverage the loan, do open an escrow account (preferably at the bank you hope to do business with) for these funds so that if you fail to secure the loan, your stockholders' money will be returned to them in full.

Banks and Bank Financing

Few books on small business financing spend much time on the process of commercial lending and lending practices. Some authors go as far as trying to teach you how to outwit or even bully a banker. They paint the banker as uncaring, stingy, and stupid. I must admit there are lousy bankers just as there are lousy entrepreneurs; but if you approach a bank with the attitude that you must beat the money out of them, you're going to have a rough time indeed. Commercial banks, usually the ones with "national" in their names, make most of their money from sound business loans. Of course, they want that loan secured by collateral, but they don't want the hassle of going after that security in the case of default; they're never certain they'll get their money back. They want the loan repaid in accordance with its provisions. That's only fair to them and it's the best deal for you as well. If the loan has fixed payments over some period of time, you plan that as a fixed cost of doing business. No other cost you have will stay that uniform.

We're going to look at what banks are looking for and what turns them off. Remember one thing: banks are run by people—they hope, they fear, they laugh, they cry. A banker probably worries about his checkbook balance or wants her children to succeed in school. They have their operating rules just as you have yours.

What Do Banks Look For?

A bank is a very special kind of creditor, always looking for the "six C's" of credit:

1. *Character.* Who's borrowing this money? Businesses don't borrow and repay money, people do. If you seriously ran afoul of the law; if you defaulted on past obligations; if your overall reputation is in question, you probably face an uphill battle. Bankers also assess you as a person. Do you seem to know what you're doing? Are you enthusiastic about your new business? Do you demonstrate confidence?

2. *Cause.* What is the money being used for? What type of business? Every bank has its own list of no-no's. One kind of no-no pertains to how the money will be used. You can't just borrow money, stick it in the corporate checkbook, and pay yourself some extravagant salary. Remember the application-of-funds part of the business plan? Banks understand that some money must stay in the form of cash, but most of it should go for real things—renovations, equipment, inventory. The other no-no involves the type of business. Although you may find some variation from bank to bank, most lending institutions stay away from:
   a. Startups that propose multiple locations. You're going to have a hard enough time getting one establishment off the ground, never mind two or more.
   b. Too much of one thing. You need to consider a diversified product line, a diversified market, or both.
   c. Fads. No one ever knows for sure whether something will catch on or die away, but if your business looks transient, a bank will back off.
   d. High-risk businesses. This list changes from time to time but usually includes bars, independent truckers, real estate developers, building contractors, gas stations, high fashion stores.
   e. Any business which borders on the unethical or even the immoral. I do know a commercial banker who backed a massage parlor, but that's rare. Bankers are a conservative lot by nature.
   Some banks won't finance startups at all because of the high risks involved.

3. *Capacity.* This refers to the capacity of the borrower to repay the loan. In a small business, a person pays off the loan, not the business. If you worked your loan repayment (also called debt service) into your cash flow projections, you've demonstrated how repayment fits in with income and other expenses.

   Most bankers feel the biggest borrowing shortcoming on the part of entrepreneurs is the failure to answer the question, "How will this loan be repaid?"

   Because the loan repayment must be made from sales, most bankers will ask how you arrived at your projected sales total. If your marketing research is sound, you have a ready, logical, defendable answer. You may also have to face the fact that there are bankers who simply refuse to accept your figures.

4. *Collateral.* Unless you're related to J. Paul Getty, no bank will grant an unsecured loan for a startup. You must show how your loan will be secured (collateralized).
5. *Capital.* What is the net worth of the borrower? How much capital is the entrepreneur putting into the business? What other equity capital is being supplied? By whom?
6. *Conditions.* As you know, the economy is always changing. During the early 1980's, business loans were difficult to secure and interest rates were hovering around 20 percent. When credit loosens up, banks become more competitive, capital is easier to come by, and it's cheaper.

In addition to the "six C's," the additional business considerations that help sway a bank are:

... a demonstrated need for the business. Although the present market may be reaching saturation, a computer retail store in the early 1980's certainly meets this criterion;
... established guidelines. Naturally, any well-established franchise (McDonald's, Culligan, Pizza Hut) can point to a high degree of success because it isn't selling, say, a clever way to make hamburgers, but a proven management method;
... a guarantee over and beyond collateral. This could be a co-signer to your loan who is reasonably well-off, or it could be a loan guarantor like the SBA.

What banks look for in the entrepreneur is:

... someone who's truly committed to and enthusiastic about the business. Good bankers can easily spot folks on an ego trip.
... a person who appears to be smart and logical. You don't have to be the resident genius but you must demonstrate you know what you're talking about. The business must be realistic and not blue-sky dreaming.
... experience. There are two kinds of experience: general business knowledge and a background in the type of business you're starting. Having neither probably dooms your loan approval. One is fine. Both are great! Financial experience is especially prized.

Things that *absolutely* turn a bank off include:

... a poor personal credit history. This doesn't mean simply missing a payment here and there. However, if you've had a car repossessed, a mortgage foreclosed, or if you've been through business or personal bankruptcy, it's going to be tough. On a lesser scale, judgments against you or liens on any of your assets can also cloud the issue.
... a criminal record. I personally disagree with this attitude, but it exists nonetheless. Of course, the nature of the crime and nature of the sentence, if any, do enter in. It's one thing if you were detained in the slammer for one night for some domestic issue but quite another if you embezzled bank funds.
... no cash. If you have no equity whatsoever, either personal or invested by others, forget it.

Getting Ready to Go to the Bank

Your preparation for your meeting with a commercial loan officer is more important than the actual meeting itself. Bankers tell me they're appalled at the number of people who wander in off the street without an appointment, with little or no preparation, and ask for a business loan. This approach might work with a loan shark, but don't *ever* try it with a bank. You'll get a quick and possibly not so polite refusal. Respect the banker and show him or her normal business courtesies.

If you don't already have a relationship with a commercial bank, you need to target your choice. Your accountant can suggest one or two banks and you can also ask other entrepreneurs. Pick your first choice and one or two as backup. First obtain the name and title of the appropriate officer who handles commercial loans for startups. In very small banks this may be the president. In medium-size banks you'll probably be referred to one of the commercial loan officers, possibly even the head of the commercial loan department. In larger banks, it may be the manager of the branch bank nearest you. In some cases you may wind up with a junior officer, but it's important to deal with the designated person. If you jump the chain of command within the bank, you may harm your case right from the beginning.

Regarding dealing with more than one bank: "Shopping the loan" should be done only under certain conditions and then with care. Bankers tell me that if you have "the deal of the century" then you're probably well-advised to go to several banks *BUT* make sure you inform each banker about the others. If you have some phenomenal situation, you can look for the most favorable terms and may even engage in a little negotiating (notice I said negotiating, not holding an auction) between banks. If your situation is average or marginal, shopping only hurts. A banker's attitude is, "Since this deal isn't the most attractive, why should I spend all the time processing the loan application only to have some other bank take it. The heck with it."

The next step is for *you* (not your accountant and especially not your attorney) to call the proper person at the bank. Introduce yourself, talk briefly about the business and the amount of money you need. Be certain the banker knows this is a startup and neither the purchase of a going concern nor a business expansion. You may get turned down on the phone; if that happens, ask the person if he or she has any suggestions. Thank them for their time.

If you get an appointment, *ask* the officer if it's O.K. to bring along your accountant and/or partner (limit it to one if there are more). *DO NOT* bring your attorney, and *never* bring more than three people. Bankers tell me lawyers only muddy up the first meeting because they often zealously attempt to overprotect their client. Banks have certain issues they won't budge on, and having a lawyer sit there arguing extraneous details only slows the process, frustrates the banker, and costs you money to boot. It may also kill the deal.

Tell the banker you have a business plan and ask what else you should bring. Bankers vary considerably on this. If this is the first meeting, it may be a get-acquainted session or what one bank president calls "mutual seduction." Chances are, though, the banker may also want:

> ... copies of your income tax returns for the past three years;
> ... your business lease agreement if you've signed one;
> ... insurance documents (life, casualty);
> ... some bank forms filled out in advance: e.g., a personal financial statement. See the next two pages for a widely used form. The bank is especially interested in credit references and your social security number;
> ... a list of collateral, including market values of homes, stocks, bonds;
> ... the personal financial statement of anyone acting as co-signer or loan guarantor;
> ... certificate of incorporation (if corporation), partnership agreement (if partnership);
> ... a list of investors (stockholders, limited partners) showing amounts of investment;
> ... samples of your products (manufacturing and retail only).

PERSONAL FINANCIAL STATEMENT

IMPORTANT: Read these directions before completing this Statement.

☐ If you are applying for individual credit in your own name and are relying on your own income or assets and not the income or assets of another person as the basis for repayment of the credit requested, complete only Sections 1 and 3.

☐ If you are applying for joint credit with another person, complete all Sections providing information in Section 2 about the joint applicant.

☐ If you are applying for individual credit, but are relying on income from alimony, child support, or separate maintenance or on the income or assets of another person as a basis for repayment of the credit requested, complete all Sections, providing information in Section 2 about the person whose alimony, support, or maintenance payments or income or assets you are relying.

☐ If this statement relates to your guaranty of the indebtedness of other person(s), firm(s) or corporation(s), complete Sections 1 and 3.

TO:

SECTION 1 - INDIVIDUAL INFORMATION (Type or Print)	SECTION 2 - OTHER PARTY INFORMATION (Type or Print)
Name	Name
Residence Address	Residence Address
City, State & Zip	City, State & Zip
Position or Occupation	Position or Occupation
Business Name	Business Name
Business Address	Business Address
City, State & Zip	City, State & Zip
Res. Phone Bus. Phone	Res. Phone Bus. Phone

SECTION 3 - STATEMENT OF FINANCIAL CONDITION AS OF _____ 19 ____

ASSETS (Do not include Assets of doubtful value)	In Dollars (Omit cents)		LIABILITIES	In Dollars (Omit cents)	
Cash on hand and in banks			Notes payable to banks - secured		
U.S. Gov't. & Marketable Securities - see Schedule A			Notes payable to banks - unsecured		
Non-Marketable Securities - See Schedule B			Due to brokers		
Securities held by broker in margin accounts			Amounts payable to others - secured		
Restricted or control stocks			Amounts payable to others - unsecured		
Partial interest in Real Estate Equities - see Schedule C			Accounts and bills due		
			Unpaid income tax		
Real Estate Owned - see Schedule D			Other unpaid taxes and interest		
Loans Receivable			Real estate mortgages payable - see Schedule D		
Automobiles and other personal property					
Cash value-life insurance-see Schedule E			Other debts - itemize:		
Other assets - itemize:					
			TOTAL LIABILITIES		
			NET WORTH		
TOTAL ASSETS			TOTAL LIAB. AND NET WORTH		

SOURCES OF INCOME FOR YEAR ENDED _____, 19____		PERSONAL INFORMATION
Salary, bonuses & commissions	$	Do you have a will?_____ if so, name of executor.
Dividends		
Real estate income		Are you a partner or officer in any other venture? If so, describe.
Other income (**Alimony, child support, or separate maintenance**		
income need not be revealed if you do not wish to have it		Are you obligated to pay alimony, child support or separate maintenance payments? If so, describe.
considered as a basis for repaying this obligation)		
		Are any assets pledged other than as described on schedules? If so, describe.
TOTAL	$	

CONTINGENT LIABILITIES		
Do you have any contingent liabilities? If so, describe.		Income tax settled through (date)_____
		Are you a defendant in any suits or legal actions?
As indorser, co-maker or guarantor?	$	Personal bank accounts carried at:
On leases or contracts?	$	
Legal claims	$	
Other special debt	$	Have you ever been declared bankrupt? If so, describe.
Amount of contested income tax liens	$	

(COMPLETE SCHEDULES AND SIGN ON REVERSE SIDE)

SCHEDULE A - U.S. GOVERNMENTS & MARKETABLE SECURITIES

Number of Shares or Face Value (Bonds)	Description	In Name Of	Are These Pledged?	Market Value

SCHEDULE B - NON-MARKETABLE SECURITIES

Number of Shares	Description	In Name Of	Are These Pledged?	Source of Value	Value

SCHEDULE C - PARTIAL INTERESTS IN REAL ESTATE EQUITIES

Address & Type Of Property	Title In Name Of	% Of Ownership	Date Acquired	Cost	Market Value	Mortgage Maturity	Mortgage Amount

SCHEDULE D - REAL ESTATE OWNED

Address & Type Of Property	Title In Name Of	Date Acquired	Cost	Market Value	Mortgage Maturity	Mortgage Amount

SCHEDULE E - LIFE INSURANCE CARRIED, INCLUDING N.S.L.I. AND GROUP INSURANCE

Name Of Insurance Company	Owner Of Policy	Beneficiary	Face Amount	Policy Loans	Cash Surrender Value

SCHEDULE F - BANKS OR FINANCE COMPANIES WHERE CREDIT HAS BEEN OBTAINED

Name & Address Of Lender	Credit In The Name Of	Secured Or Unsecured?	Original Date	High Credit	Current Balance

(USE ADDITIONAL SCHEDULES IF NECESSARY)

The information contained in this statement is provided for the purpose of obtaining, or maintaining credit with you on behalf of the undersigned, or persons, firms or corporations in whose behalf the undersigned may either severally or jointly with others, execute a guaranty in your favor. Each undersigned understands that you are relying on the information provided herein (including the designation made as to ownership of property) in deciding to grant or continue credit. Each undersigned represents and warrants that the information provided is true and complete and that you may consider this statement as continuing to be true and correct until a written notice of a change is given to you by the undersigned. You are authorized to make all inquiries you deem necessary to verify the accuracy of the statements made herein, and to determine my/our creditworthiness. You are authorized to answer questions about your credit experience with me/us.

Signature (Individual) _____

S.S. No _____ Date of Birth _____

Signature (Other Party) _____

S.S. No _____ Date of Birth _____

Date Signed_____ 19_____

Be certain to allow enough time to do this homework before the appointment. A sample way to list collateral is shown below.

COLLATERAL OFFERED FOR A LOAN FOR
DICK'S CYCLE SHOP, INC.

Item	Market Value
1. Single-family residence located at 23 Elm Street, first mortgage held by Consumer Savings Bank. Mortgage balance on 6/1/xx, $27,324.97 Property appraised by Robert Scranton, MAI, 6/10/xx	$42,500.00
2. Fifty common shares of IBM Corp. Value taken at closing 6/8/xx, 102-¼	5,112.50
3. Opening inventory—bicycles and parts. Value at cost on opening day	18,900.00
4. Equipment (at cost):	
a. Machines and tools	6,200.00
b. Furniture and fixtures	2,300.00
c. Cash register	1,895.00
Total	$76,907.50

Let's look at the collateral for Dick's Cycle Shop and see how a bank might evaluate it. I say "might" because things vary from time to time and bank to bank.

1. *The house.* First, the bank determines the equity in the home by subtracting the mortgage balance from the market value:

$$\begin{array}{r} \$42,500.00 \\ -27,324.97 \\ \hline \$15,175.03 \end{array}$$

   By taking some part of the balance, usually between 70 and 90 percent, the actual value to the bank is determined. We'll use 80 percent and round off results to the nearest dollar.

   80% × $15,175.03 . . . . $12,140.00

2. *The stock.* IBM is considered a "blue chip" security and therefore the bank accepts 75 percent of its total value for collateral. The value is lower on less stable securities and higher for U.S. government obligations (notes, bonds, bills).

   75% × $5112.50   3,834.00

3. *Inventory.* 50 percent of the total is normal figure used.

   50% × $18,900.00   9,450.00

4. *Equipment.*

		Market Value
a. Machines and tools:	60% × $6,200.00	3,720.00
b. Furniture & fixtures:	40% × $2,300.00	920.00
c. Cash register:	70% × $1,895.00	1,327.00
Total		$31,391.00

Our cycling entrepreneur can probably secure a $30,000 loan with his collateral.

Other collateral includes:

  . . . mortgages on business real estate;
  . . . warehouse receipts (items placed in a public warehouse);
  . . . trust receipts for floor planning (used for items such as appliances; boats, automobiles, power equipment);

... accounts receivable;
... life insurance if it has cash surrender value;
... savings accounts;
... the guarantee of another person (e.g., a wealthy individual who may also be a stockholder; your parents).

You can't collateralize things like irrevocable trusts or the fact that you're mentioned in Uncle Harold's will.

There are two other things to do before the meeting. One is to be sure of your attitude. Be positive about the outcome of the meeting (even if you don't get the loan), your business idea and proposition, and most of all, yourself. Remember, you're presenting a situation that's mutually profitable to you and to the bank, monetarily and otherwise.

The second thing is to be sure your presentation is clear, logical, and concise. Don't memorize a "pitch" but think through what you want to say. You'll be asked probing questions such as:

... What makes you think this business will make it?
... What will you do if a new competitor opens up?
... Why have you chosen this location?
... Who are your employees? Suppliers? Customers?
... What business experience do you have?

The Meeting Itself   It's the big day! You're going to meet a person whose dual dedication is (1) to help people in small business, and (2) to maintain the financial integrity of his or her business. A balance must exist for a bank or the bank ceases to exist. If you've done your homework, the meeting will be a piece of cake. You'll be miles ahead of most others competing for the bank's money.

Be certain to dress for the occasion; a business suit is best.

Remember, *you* make the presentation. If your accountant is present, he or she can answer questions but not make any lengthy discourse.

After the presentation and any questions, one of three things will happen:

... you'll be turned down;
... you'll be asked to provide more information;
... you'll be told that the bank will consider the deal.

If you are turned down, it may be the best advice you could get. You have the right to ask two questions:

1. Why was I turned down?
2. What do I have to do to get the loan?

Listen carefully to both answers. By all means, don't walk out in a huff. Thank the banker honestly for his time and advice and either look for another bank or begin making the necessary changes.

If you're asked for more information (detailed resumé, loan application form, financial data), tell the banker when he or she can expect to have it. There is a sample of a typical business application form on the next two pages.

APPLICATION
Small Business Term Loan

TO: THE FIRST NATIONAL BANK OF ANYTOWN.   Date ....

The undersigned hereby submit(s) application for a loan in the net amount of

....Dollars $ [   ]

For the purpose of ....

....

....

to be repaid in .... monthly payments on the ☐5th ☐10th ☐15th ☐20th ☐25th ☐30th day of the month.

BUSINESS RECORD   ☐ Corporation
                                       ☐ Partnership

Name of Business .... ☐ Proprietorship
                                (Please Print)

Kind of Business ....Phone No. ....

Address...
              (Street)   (City or Town)   (Zone)   (State)
Year Business Established ....Annual Rent $ ....Lease Expires ....

Business Checking Account ....
                                (Name of Bank)

PRINCIPALS

Name.. Date of Birth ....

Residence ....

Residence Telephone No. .... No. of years at present residence .... Number of Dependents ....

Previous Residence ....

Checking a/c (bank) .... Title of account .... Balance $ ....

Savings or Cooperative a/c (bank) .... a/c no .... Balance $ ....

Real Estate Owned .... Date Purchased .... Mtge. held by ....
                          Original   Present   Monthly   Rental
Cost $ ....Valuation $ .....Mortgage $ ..... Balance $ ....Payments $ ......Income $ ....

Life Insurance: Face Amt. Carried $ .... Cash Value $ .... Subject to Loan of $ ....

Other Assets: Securities Mkt. Value $ .... Auto (Make & Year) ....

Open loans To Whom Owed   Original Amount   Unpaid Balance   Monthly Payment   Collateral

.... $ .... $ .... $ ....

.... $ .... $ .... $ ....

Name .... Date of Birth ....

Residence ....

Residence Telephone No. .... No. of years at present residence ...... Number of Dependents ....

Previous Residence ....

Checking a/c (bank) .... Title of account .... Balance $ ....

Savings or Cooperative a/c (bank) .... a/c no .... Balance $ ....

Real Estate Owned .... Date Purchased .... Mtge. held by ....
                          Original   Present   Monthly   Rental
Cost $ ....Valuation $ .....Mortgage $ ..... Balance $ ....Payments $ ......Income $ ....

Life Insurance: Face Amt. Carried $ .... Cash Value $ .... Subject to Loan of $ ....

Other Assets: Securities Mkt. Value $ .... Auto (Make & Year) ....

Open loans To Whom Owed   Original Amount   Unpaid Balance   Monthly Payment   Collateral

.... $ .... $ .... $ ....

.... $ .... $ .... $ ....

Borrower, in consideration of Bank making the loan to Borrower, hereby warrants, represents and agrees as follows:

1. If Borrower is a corporation, Borrower is duly organized and existing under the laws of....................
and is duly qualified as a foreign corporation in the States of ....

2. Borrower will cause the following present indebtedness of Borrower to be subordinated to the loan by a Subordination Agreement satisfactory to Bank.

Name of Creditor of Borrower   *Amount*

....

....

....

....

3. The execution, delivery and performance hereof and any security instruments or guarantees called for or delivered hereunder are (if Borrower is a corporation) within its corporate powers, have been duly authorized, are not in contravention of the terms of Borrower's Articles of Incorporation or By-laws or any amendment thereof and (whether or not Borrower is a corporation) are not in contravention of law or of any indenture, agreement or undertaking to which Borrower is a party or by which Borrower is bound.

4. All financial statements, profit and loss statements, statements as to ownership and other statements heretofore or hereafter given to bank in connection with this agreement are or will be true and correct subject to any limitation stated therein and Borrower is the owner of all property in which Borrower has given or is giving a security interest to Bank, free from all encumbrances and Borrower will so own all property in which Borrower hereafter gives a security interest to Bank.

5. Borrower will maintain executive personnel and management satisfactory to Bank.

6. Borrower will maintain adequate fire (including so-called extended coverage), public liability and other insurance as Bank may require, in such form and written by such companies as may be satisfactory to Bank and will upon request of Bank deliver to it the policies concerned. All policies covering property given as security for the loan shall have a loss payable clause in favor of Bank.

GENERAL INFORMATION

Has the business, or any of the principals ever been involved in any judgments, attachments or other legal proceedings other than divorce, custody, alimony or separate support proceedings?

□ Yes   □ No   If "yes" attach memorandum giving details.

Name of Accountant:.. Tel. No. ....

Address: ....

Name of Insurance Agent:... Tel. No. ....

Address: ....

The foregoing statements and any supplementary information are warranted by the undersigned to be true and are furnished to induce you to make the loan applied for, which, if made, will be used only for the purpose above stated.

The Bank is authorized to obtain from any source any information which it may require to enable or assist it to pass upon this application. If this application is approved, I also authorize the Bank to give credit information to others.

The undersigned knows that you rely and will continue to rely theron until written notice of any change therein is received by you. The undersigned will give you immediate written notice of any material change in the undersigned's financial condition, including any law-suit, begun or threatened, the effect of which may be to materially alter the said condition.

The undersigned will furnish you with such financial statements and data at such times and with such certifications as you may require, without expense to you. You, and your agents and accountants, may at any time inspect the undersigned's books and accounts.

This application shall remain in the property of the Bank, whether approved, not approved, withdrawn, or if the loan is paid.

Signed this   day of   , 19

It is unlawful to deny or stop credit or services   .... (SEAL)
or to damage anyone's credit standing because of his or   Name of applicant
her sex or marital status.

By ....
                                                            Title, if any

By ....
                                                            Title, if any

If you're told to wait, ask when you can expect a final answer. The normal time is two weeks, but it could take longer. The bank will check your personal background and analyze your proposal. If the analysis is satisfactory, your proposal is presented at the weekly meeting of the loan committee. The decision of that committee depends on:

... the soundness of your proposal;
... data the bank has generated studying your proposal;
... conditions in the local economy;
... the number of loans outstanding, especially in your kind of business;
... the bank's cash position;
... current government policies on loans.

If all is positive, you get your loan. A truly professional banker may suggest additional financing, either an increase in the loan or a line of credit, which is an already approved loan that you don't use unless you need to.

There are some bankers who still think it's necessary to talk someone down on a loan. This isn't the same as an honest banker who analyzes your cash flow projections and finds errors in either judgment or arithmetic and tells you your loan request is excessive. I'm speaking of an arbitrary reduction for no sound reason. Don't go for this; it can only spell disaster. If your business plan is done carefully, it shows what you need. Taking less only causes the business to fail. You're not haggling over a used car.

Final Stages

If you're turned down after the analysis period, always ask why and what needs to be changed. If you're approved, it may be conditional, which means the bank may want something else such as an SBA guarantee. Other conditions can include:

... more equity financing;
... more collateral or personal guarantees;
... a bit more homework.

If you're totally approved, you need to go back to the bank to sign documents and discuss the final arrangements of the loan itself. See the following pages for sample loan agreement and security (collateral) agreement. Your banker may suggest something other than a term loan on a fixed repayment schedule. You may hear words like variable interest rate, balloon payments, chattel mortages. Be certain to ask questions about things you don't understand and be doubly certain you understand when payments are to be made, how much they are, what interest rate(s) you may be paying. I use the word "rate(s)" because the bank may propose one loan against inventory, another against real estate, a third against equipment, all with different interest rates and terms. Don't let this dismay you. The bank knows what it's doing. On page 85 I have a list of questions to ask before signing your name to anything.

BUSINESS LOAN AGREEMENT

TO: THE FIRST NATIONAL BANK OF ANYTOWN.

The undersigned _____
_____ (hereinafter called "Borrower") hereby ap-
plies to THE FIRST NATIONAL BANK OF ANYTOWN (hereinafter called "Bank") for a loan
(hereinafter called the "loan") to be evidenced by a promissory note which includes the following provisions or such other provisions as to which Borrower and Bank may agree in writing:

Amount of Note: $_____ Date of Note: _____

_____, 19_____

Payable: _____

Borrower, in consideration of Bank making the loan to Borrower, hereby warrants,
represents and agrees as follows:

1. The business operations of Borrower are as follows: _____
(Insert type of business, i.e.,

_____ and said business is a _____
machine shop, bakery, etc.)   *(Indicate whether sole ownership, partnership, corporation or trust)*

2. Borrower will continue said business, will not engage in any other business without permission of Bank, and will use the proceeds of the loan only in connection with said
business and for the following purposes:

3. Borrower's balance sheet as at _____

_____ 19_____ and the related statement of income and retained earnings for Borrower's
fiscal year ending on such date, both of which have been delivered to Bank, are complete and
correct and have been prepared in accordance with generally accepted accounting principles
consistently applied throughout the period involved. There are no liabilities of Borrower contingent or otherwise not disclosed in said balance sheet and since the date of such balance
sheet there has been no change in the assets, liabilities, financial condition or business of Borrower shown thereon other than changes in the ordinary course of business, the effect of
which has not been in the aggregate materially adverse.

4. So long as any amount remains unpaid under the loan:

4.1 Borrower's current business assets will exceed Borrower's current business liabilities, both determined in accordance with generally accepted accounting principles consistent
with those applied in preparation of the financial statements referred to in Paragraph 3, by at
least _____

_____ Dollars ($_____). If left blank, this provision is not applicable.

4.2 Borrower's current ratio (the relationship of current assets to current liabilities)
will be maintained at not less than   . Classification of current assets and current liabilities shall be computed in accordance with generally accepted accounting principles consistently applied.

4.3 Borrower's debt to tangible net worth ratio (the relationship of current and total
indebtedness to tangible net worth) shall not exceed
                      . For purposes of this Agreement, "tangible net worth" shall
mean the aggregate book value of the assets of the Borrower (after deduction therefrom of all
applicable reserves and allowances) minus (a) total liabilities, (b) any write-up in the value of
assets occurring after the date hereof, and (c) all intangibles including but not limited to
goodwill, leasehold improvements, patents, trademarks and the like.

4.4 Borrower's tangible net worth will not be less than $

4.5 Borrower will maintain compensating demand deposit account balances of
at least _____ of the outstanding loan bal-
ance. If such balances are not maintained, Borrower will be charged a deficiency fee equal in
amount to the product of (X) the difference between the required compensating balance and
the balance maintained, and (Y) the rate stated in the note of even date herewith for the number of days actually elapsed based on a 360 day year.

4.6 Borrower will furnish to Bank within ninety days after the close of each fiscal
year of Borrower, a balance sheet of Borrower as of the close of such year and an income

statement and statement of retained earnings for such year for Borrower (or if Borrower is an individual, for Borrower's business) certified by independent public accountants satisfactory to Bank; will furnish to Bank unaudited balance sheet and operating figures for each _____ _____ within thirty days after the end of each of said periods, and such other data as Bank may request; and will at all times permit representatives of Bank to inspect and make extracts from Borrower's books and records.

4.7 Borrower will maintain its books and records relating to its financial affairs at all times in accordance with, and all financial statements provided for herein shall be prepared in accordance with, generally accepted accounting principles consistent with those applied in preparation of the financial statements referred to in Paragraph 3.

4.8 Borrower will not pay any dividends on any class of capital stock or make any other distribution or payment on account of or in redemption of capital stock, or permit any withdrawals from or distributions of the assets of Borrower, or if Borrower is an individual, the business assets of Borrower, except as salary or compensation for services rendered after the date hereof; provided, however, that total payment for services rendered (in cash or otherwise and including dividends, withdrawals, distributions, salary and compensation) in any month to the following may equal but shall not exceed the following amounts:

Name	Monthly Amount

4.9 Borrower will maintain financially sound and reputable insurers, insurance with respect to Borrower's properties and business against such casualties and contingencies and in such types and such amounts as shall be in accordance with sound business practices.

4.10 Without the prior written consent of Bank, Borrower will not:

4.10.1 Incur, assume or permit to exist indebtedness for borrowed money except from the bank.

4.10.2 Sell, factor or borrow on the security of Borrower's accounts receivable with or without recourse, guaranty, endorse (other than for collection or deposit in the regular course of business) or become or remain liable in respect of any indebtedness, obligation or liability of any other person, firm or corporation or permit any such secondary responsibility to exist.

4.10.3 Create or permit to exist any mortgage, pledge or other lien or encumbrance on any of Borrower's property except (i) those arising from attachments or similar proceedings, pending litigation, judgments or taxes or assessments whose validity or amount is currently being contested in good faith by appropriate proceedings and for which adequate reserves have been established and maintained in accordance with generally accepted accounting principles, or taxes and assessments which are not due and delinquent; (ii) liens of carriers, warehousemen, mechanics and materialmen and other like; (iii) pledges or deposits made in connection with workmen's compensation, unemployment or other insurance, old age pensions or other social security benefits, and good faith deposits in connection with tenders, contracts or leases to which Borrower is a party, or deposits to secure, or in lieu of, surety, penalty or appeal bonds, performance bonds and other similar obligations; (iv) encumbrances consisting of easements, rights of way, zoning restrictions, restrictions on the use of real property and similar encumbrances and minor irregularities in title; (v) landlord's liens under leases; and (vi) in favor of Bank.

4.10.4 Purchase or acquire any securities of or make any loans or advances to or investments in any person, firm or corporation except obligations of the United States government or any agency of the United States government or certificates of deposit issued by any one of the fifty largest banks in the United States.

4.10.5 Merge or consolidate or sell or dispose of all or a portion of Borrower's assets other than in the ordinary course of business, or in any way or manner alter Borrower's capital structure, including the sale, transfer or redemption of any shares of the Borrower.

4.10.6 Hire or discharge any officer or retain the services of any independent contractor or professional, except in the ordinary course of business and only where the management of the Borrower is not materially affected or changed.

4.10.7 In any twelve month period spend or become obligated to spend any sum in excess of _____

Dollars ($_____) for the acquisition, construction or installation of properties to be carried in Borrower's books as fixed assets. If left blank, this provision is not applicable.

4.10.8 Incur or assume rental obligations for any current or future period of twelve consecutive months under leases of real or personal property aggregating more than $_____ or

aggregating more than $_____

_____ at any one time outstanding.

5. The loan and any and all other obligations of Borrower to Bank, direct or indirect, absolute or contingent, due or to become due, now existing or hereafter arising (the "Obligations") shall at Bank's option become immediately due and payable without notice or demand at any time after (a) default in the payment or performance of any Obligation; (b) default in the observance by Borrower of any of the terms of this Agreement; (c) death, dissolution, termination of existence, insolvency, business failure, appointment of a receiver of any part of the property of, assignment for the benefit of creditors by, or the commencement of any proceedings under any bankruptcy or insolvency laws by or against Borrower or any party secondarily liable under any of the Obligations.

6. Any deposits or other sums at any time credited by or due from Bank to Borrower and any securities or other property of Borrower in Bank's possession may at all times be held and treated as security for payment of the Obligations. In the event any one or more of the events of default set forth in Paragraph 5 shall have occurred or be continuing, then regardless of the adequacy of any collateral, any deposits or other sums credited by or due from Bank to Borrower may be set off against any and all of the Obligations.

7. Borrower will at all times execute and deliver such further instruments and take such further action as may reasonably be requested by Bank in order to carry out the intent and purposes of this Agreement.

8. No failure or delay on Bank's part in exercising any right hereunder shall operate as a waiver thereof or any other right. No waiver hereunder shall be effective unless in writing and a waiver on any one occasion shall not be a waiver of any right or remedy on any future occasion.

9. In case of a default in the performance of the Obligations, Borrower will pay to Bank such further amount as shall be sufficient to cover the cost and expense of collection including (without limitation) reasonable attorneys' fees and expenses.

10. This Agreement shall be deemed to be a sealed contract under the law of (state) and shall be construed in accordance with such law.

11. Borrower agrees to additional provisions as follows:

_____

_____

_____

_____

_____

_____

_____

_____

_____

_____

IN WITNESS WHEREOF, Borrower has executed and delivered this Loan Agreement this _____

day of _____, 19_____.

_____

_____

SECURITY AGREEMENT

_____

NAME

_____

STREET AND NUMBER   CITY   STATE

(hereinafter called "Debtor"), hereby grants to THE FIRST NATIONAL BANK OF ANYTOWN (hereinafter called "Bank"), to secure the payment of $_____ as provided in the Debtor's note(s) of even date herewith and also to secure the payment and performance of all other obligations of Debtor to Bank, whether direct or indirect, absolute or contingent, due or to become due, now existing or hereafter arising (all of the foregoing, including said notes, being hereinafter called the "Obligations"), a security interest in the following personal property of Debtor and any and all additions, substitutions, accessions and proceeds thereto or thereof (all of the same being hereinafter called the "Collateral"):

Debtor hereby warrants and covenants that—

1. The Collateral will be kept at _____ until such time as written consent to a change of location is obtained from Bank.

2. Except for the security interest granted hereby, Debtor is the owner of the Collateral free from all encumbrances and will defend the same against the claims and demands of all persons. Debtor will not pledge, mortgage or create, or suffer to exist, a security interest in the Collateral in favor of any person other than Bank, and will not sell or transfer the Collateral or any interest therein without the prior written consent of Bank.

3. The Collateral shall remain personal property irrespective of the manner of its attachment to any real estate. If the Collateral is attached to real estate prior to the perfection of the security interest granted hereby, Debtor will on demand of Bank furnish to Bank a disclaimer or disclaimers, signed by all persons having an interest in the real estate, of any interest in the Collateral which is prior to Bank's interest. Debtor will notify Bank in writing of any intended sale, mortgage or conveyancy of any real estate to which the Collateral is at any time attached, and will give written notice of the terms and conditions of this agreement to any prospective purchaser, mortgagee, grantee or other transferee of the real estate or any interest therein.

4. Debtor will immediately notify Bank in writing of any change in address from that shown in this agreement, shall at all reasonable times and from time to time allow Bank, by or through any of its officers, agents, attorneys or accountants, to examine, inspect or make extracts from Debtor's books and records, and shall do, make, execute and deliver all such additional and further acts, things, deeds, assurances and instruments as Bank may require more completely to vest in and assure to Bank its rights hereunder or in any of the Collateral.

5. Debtor will keep the Collateral at all times insured by such insurance as Bank may from time to time require, and in any event and without specific request by Bank, will insure the Collateral against fire, including so-called extended coverage, theft, and, in the case of any motor vehicle, collision, all insurance to be with such insurance companies as Bank shall approve, with loss thereon to be payable to Bank and Debtor as their respective interests may appear. All policies of insurance shall provide for not less than ten days' notice of cancellation or change in form to Bank and, if requested by Bank, shall be delivered to and held by it until all of the Obligations have been fully performed.

6. Debtor will keep the Collateral in good order and repair, and will not use the same in violation of law or any policy of insurance thereon. Bank may inspect the Collateral at any reasonable time, wherever located. Debtor will pay promptly when due all taxes and assessments upon the Collateral or for its use or operation or upon this agreement.

7. In its discretion, Bank may discharge taxes and other encumbrances at any time levied or placed on the Collateral, make repairs, thereof and place and pay for insurance thereon and pay any necessary filing fees. Debtor agrees to reimburse Bank on demand for any and all expenditures so made, and until paid the amount thereof shall be a debt secured by the Collateral. Bank shall have no obligation to Debtor to make any such expenditures nor shall the making thereof relieve Debtor of any default. Bank

may act as attorney for Debtor in making, adjusting and settling claims under any insurance covering the Collateral.

8. Debtor may have possession and use of the Collateral until default. Upon the happening of any of the following events or conditions, namely: (a) default in the payment or performance of any of the Obligations, of any liability or obligation to Bank of any indorser, guarantor or surety of or for any of the Obligations, or of any covenant or liability contained or referred to herein or in any note, instrument, document or agreement evidencing any Obligation; (b) any representation or warranty of Debtor in this agreement or made to Bank by Debtor to induce it to enter into this agreement or to make a loan to Debtor proving false or erroneous in any material respect; (c) loss, theft, material damage, destruction, sale, or encumbrance of or to the Collateral, or the making of any levy thereon or seizure or attachment thereof by legal process; (d) death, dissolution, termination of existence, insolvency, business failure, appointment of a receiver of any part of the property of, assignment for the benefit of creditors by, or the commencement of any proceeding under any bankruptcy or insolvency laws by or against Debtor, or any indorser, guarantor or surety of or for any Obligation; (e) such a change in the management or ownership of Debtor as in the opinion of Bank increases its risk; thereupon, and as long as such default continues, Bank may without notice or demand declare all of the Obligations to be immediately due and payable, and Bank shall then have in any jurisdiction where enforcement hereof is sought, in addition to all other rights and remedies, the rights and remedies of a secured party under the Uniform Commercial Code, including without limitation thereto the right to take immediate possession of the Collateral, and for the purpose Bank may, so far as Debtor can give authority therefor, enter upon any premises on which the Collateral, or any part thereof, may be situated and remove the same therefrom. Debtor will upon demand make the Collateral available to Bank at a place and time designated by Bank which is reasonably convenient to both parties. Bank will give Debtor at least five days' prior written notice of the time and place of any public sale of the Collateral or of the time after which any private sale thereof is to be made. From the proceeds of the sale, Bank shall be entitled to retain (i) all sums secured hereby, (ii) its reasonable expenses of retaking, holding, preparing for sale and selling, and (iii) reasonable legal expenses incurred by it in connection herewith and with such sale. No waiver by Bank or any default shall be effective unless in writing nor operate as a waiver of any other default or of the same default on another occasion.

9. Debtor waives demand, notice, protest, notice of acceptance of this agreement, notice of loans made, credit extended, collateral received or delivered or other action taken in reliance hereon and all other demands and notices of any description. With respect both to the Obligations and the Collateral, Debtor assents to any extension or postponement of the time of payment or any other indulgence, to any substitution, exchange or release of collateral, to the addition or release of any party or person primarily or secondarily liable, to the acceptance of partial payment thereon and the settlement, compromising or adjusting of any thereof, all in such manner and at such time or times as Bank may deem advisable. Bank shall have no duty as to the collection or protection of the Collateral or any income thereon, nor as to the preservation of rights against prior parties, nor as to the preservation of any rights pertaining thereto beyond the safe custody thereof. Bank may exercise its rights with respect to the Collateral without resorting or regard to other collateral or sources of reimbursement for liability. Bank shall not be deemed to have waived any of its rights upon or under the Obligations or the Collateral unless such waiver be in writing and signed by Bank. No delay or omission on the part of Bank in exercising any right shall operate as a waiver of such right or any other right. A waiver on any one occasion shall not be construed as a bar to or waiver of any right on any future occasion. All rights and remedies of Bank on the Obligations or the Collateral, whether evidenced hereby or by any other instrument or papers, shall be cumulative and may be exercised separately or concurrently.

10. This agreement and all rights and obligations hereunder, including matters of construction, validity and performance, shall be governed by the law of (state). This agreement is intended to take effect as a sealed instrument.

IN WITNESS WHEREOF, Debtor has executed _____ original counterparts of this agreement on this _____

day of _____, 19____.

SIGNED AND SEALED
IN THE PRESENCE OF   _____

                                        By_____

_____
        WITNESS

LOAN CHECKLIST

Questions to Ask the Loan Officer

1. Regarding interest—what rate is it? Is it fixed or variable? If it is variable, how much can it vary? When does the interest commence? Can I pay interest only for some period?

2. What is the maturity date of the loan? Is the last payment a normal payment or is it higher?

3. What is the price of placement? (*Note:* Some banks charge "points," meaning percentage points. This is a one-time fee. If you borrow $20,000 at two points—2 percent—you will be charged $400.)

4. Do I have the right to repay the outstanding balance at any time? Is there a fee to do this?

5. Must I sign a personal guarantee for a business loan? (You will probably be required to do so.)

6. What will I be required to do other than make payments? (*Note:* You may have to maintain certain financial ratios or keep a certain minimum in your checking account, called a compensating balance.)

7. What insurances am I required to have?

8. Can the bank assign the loan to another party?

9. What am I restricted from doing? (Example: paying dividends or high salaries.)

10. What constitutes default? What will happen? What costs will be charged? What is the process with foreclosure?

Continuing Bank Relations

If you receive your loan, the worst thing you can do is never cooperate or communicate with your banker again. Bring all your business to that bank—personal checking, savings, certificates of deposit. You're in a total business relationship. Don't shortchange the deal by spreading yourself around. You want someone on your side. Be certain to send quarterly income statements and balance sheets to your banker and plan to take her or him to lunch at least twice a year to share the good news as well as the bad. Your banker doesn't want to hear bad news on the street. If it looks as though you might need additional financing, advise your banker well in advance. Bankers never respond well to what is called "Friday night financing."

In addition, don't switch banks for a couple of percentage points on a loan. You'll only do it once. If you find after a year or so that your bank isn't giving you the service you want, then look for another lending institution.

If things really get rough—sales are much lower than expected or expenses are higher than you planned—your banker will want to see you monthly. You'll have to do a new cash flow projection. If you can't make a loan payment, for goodness sake, call your banker *in advance*. Explain the situation.

If you get in trouble, you may find your banker ready to help by:

   . . . restructuring the loan;
   . . . postponing principal payments;
   . . . granting more credit;

but only if you explain what's happened and only if you show how you plan to correct the situation. Work with the bank officers and they'll work with you. They don't want to see you fail in business for several reasons:

1. It's often difficult for a bank to sell collateral and realize its investment from it.
2. A bank has expenses just as you do. If you can't meet your obligations to them, they have difficulty meeting theirs.
3. If a smaller bank makes *one* business loan at their legal limit and that loan defaults, it alone may erase their entire year's profit.
4. It becomes a black mark on their record, too.

If you succeed, so do they. It's a nice partnership. Now let's talk about the SBA.

The Small Business Administration

Let's get one thing straight from the beginning: the letters SBA do not stand for Small Business Annihilators, nor do they stand for Slowest Bastards in America. The U.S. Small Business Administration is an agency of the government chartered specifically to help small business. Although the role of the SBA changes, it has two major purposes:

1. To provide education, information, and direct management assistance (consulting) at little or no cost.
2. To guarantee bank loans made to small business owners.

The SBA does loan some money, but this is not the rule, and what little lending it does do may end soon.

Many people have heard about the SBA but are unsure what it does and how to use it. In the first place, you can use the SBA as you would a consultant to your business. Some SBA employees are management assistance officers, and you can also request the help of private individuals who are part of the SCORE or ACE programs referenced earlier in the book. A form for requesting assistance is on the next page. There is no charge for these services, except in the case of SCORE/ACE where you will be obligated for that person's travel expenses, and they are available whether or not you have SBA loan participation. Secondarily, the SBA does offer financial assistance but there is no requirement to ask for it. As a matter of fact, if you can secure traditional bank financing without the SBA's participation, you are better off because the participation only adds one more party to the picture.

I'm going to explain the SBA's role in financing. However, if you want more information, visit your nearest SBA office (See Appendix A.) and/or purchase a copy of *How to Finance Your Small Business with Government Money: SBA Loans* by R. Hayes and J. Howell (1980, John Wiley & Sons, NY).

SBA's Financial Role: Direct Loans

I mentioned that the SBA still makes a few *direct* loans but not as many as they used to. This is because, by law, the agency may not make or guarantee a loan if a business can obtain funds on reasonable terms from a bank or other private source. An entrepreneur must seek private financing before he or she applies to the SBA for a loan. So, don't go to the SBA until you talk to the bank. If two

OMB 3245-0019

SMALL BUSINESS ADMINISTRATION

REQUEST FOR MANAGEMENT ASSISTANCE

Please Print

Name of Company	Name of Inquirer	Telephone #

Street	City	State	County	Zip

Employer ID #	Social Security Number	Veteran	Viet Era Veteran
		Yes ☐ No ☐	Yes ☐ No ☐ Discharged:

Are you presently:	Yes	No	Can you furnish a recent:		Yes	No
In Business?	☐	☐	Balance Sheet?		☐	☐
Starting a Business?	☐	☐	Profit & Loss Statement?		☐	☐
SBA Borrower?	☐	☐				

Kind of business/services (Please specify)

Retail (Selling) _____   Construction _____

Service (Kind) _____   Wholesale (Selling) _____

Manufacturing (Product) _____   Other (Specify) _____

Check the problem areas for which you seek assistance.

☐ 1. Starting a New Business
☐ 2. Sources of Credit and Financing
☐ 3. Increasing Sales
☐ 4. Advertising & Sales Promotion
☐ 5. Market Research
☐ 6. Selling to the Government
☐ 7. Bidding and Estimating
☐ 8. International Trade

☐ 9. Recordkeeping and Accounting
☐ 10. Financial Statements
☐ 11. Office or Plant Management
☐ 12. Personnel
☐ 13. Engineering and Research
☐ 14. Inventory Control
☐ 15. Purchasing
☐ 16. Credit & Collections

Please describe how SBA may be of assistance.

I request management assistance from the Small Business Administration. I understand that this assistance is free of charge and that I incur no obligation to SBA or its counselor for providing this assistance. I authorize SBA to furnish relevant information to the assigned management counselor although I expect that information to be held in strict confidence by him/her.

I further understand that any counselor has agreed not to: (1) recommend goods or services from sources in which he/she has an interest and (2) accept fees or commissions developing from this counseling relationship. In consideration of SBA's furnishing management or technical assistance, I waive all claims against SBA personnel or counselors arising from this assistance.

Signature and Title of Requestor	Date

SBA Form 641 (2-82) Previous editions are obsolete

GPO 887-50

banks turn you down,* *then* you can talk to the SBA about direct financing. However, the same criteria of personal resources, collateral, and a sound business plan still apply.

Although Congress may change the rules and the financial appropriations, the SBA has had some direct loan money available for:

> . . . low income and other "disadvantaged" persons;
> . . . non-profit sheltered workshops;
> . . . handicapped persons in business;
> . . . firms engaged in certain specific energy conservation projects;
> . . . Vietnam veterans and handicapped veterans;
> . . . export purposes.

To be eligible for an SBA loan, your business must:

1. Meet certain size limitations (number of employees, sales).
2. Be independently owned and operated.
3. Be a profit-making venture (except for a non-profit sheltered workshop).
4. Not be dominant in its field. (American Motors, with 28,000 employees, once qualified for an SBA loan using this provision.)
5. Not discriminate in its employment.

SBA will not consider loans to "speculative" businesses, newspapers (don't ask me why this is), and gambling operations.

As the loan applicant, you must:

1. Be of good character.
2. Show an ability to run a business successfully.
3. Have enough personal capital at stake to withstand losses and operate on a sound financial basis.
4. Show that the proposed loan is of such a sound value or so secured as to reasonably assure payment.

Direct loans are presently limited to $150,000, except that handicapped assistance loans carry a maximum of $100,000. Regular business loans have a maximum maturity of 25 years and working capital loans are generally limited to seven years. Interest rates vary with economic conditions but are generally in line with market rates.

Collateral must be one or more of the following:

1. A mortgage on land, building.
2. A mortgage on chattels. This is a lien against assets such as cash registers and vehicles.
3. Assignment of warehouse receipts for marketable merchandise.
4. Guarantees or personal endorsements.
5. In some instances, assignment of current accounts receivable.

The SBA recommends the following steps for those wanting to start a business:

1. Describe the type of business you plan to establish.
2. Describe your experience and management capabilities.
3. Prepare an estimate of how much you or others have to invest in the business and how much you will need to borrow.

---

* This holds true in cities with populations greater than 200,000. You only need one refusal in smaller towns.

4. Prepare a current net worth statement (balance sheet) listing all personal assets and all liabilities.

5. Prepare a detailed projection of earnings for the first year the business will operate.

6. List collateral to be offered as security for the loan, indicating your estimate of the present market value of each item.

7. Take the foregoing material to your banker. Ask for a direct bank loan and if you are declined, ask the bank to make the loan under SBA's Loan Guarantee Plan. If the bank is interested in an SBA guaranteed or participation loan, ask the banker to contact SBA for discussion of your application. In most cases of guaranteed or participation loans, SBA will deal directly with the bank.

8. If a guaranteed or a participation loan is not available, write or visit the nearest SBA office. SBA has 110 field offices which often send loan officers to visit many smaller cities as need indicates. To speed matters, make your financial information available when you first write or visit the SBA.

Note that your business plan already provides much of the proper information for the SBA.

SBA's Financial Role: Guaranteed Loans

The guaranteed loan program is the one that you'll most likely use if you go the SBA route. There are advantages and disadvantages to doing so. The advantages are:

... a bank *may* be more willing to make the loan with 70 to 90 percent of it backed by a government agency. If you receive a $50,000 loan which is 90 percent guaranteed by SBA and you default, the SBA must fork over $45,000 to the bank and then come after you for reimbursement.

... the loan guarantee sometimes permits a bank to do business differently, more flexibly. For example, some states don't allow banks to take second mortgages; with SBA participation, they can.

... the bank *may* be more willing to use a fixed interest rate—say two and a half points over the prime interest rate—rather than a rate that fluctuates. The fixed rate is generally preferred by business owners because they can plan their interest expense in advance rather than get a monthly interest bill which is constantly changing.

... if you run into financial difficulty, the SBA may help in re-negotiating the loan. You're dealing with an agency of the U.S. government which has wide experience with small business, especially its problems. Sometimes a banker and an entrepreneur may disagree or even become hostile to one another; the SBA can help.

Disadvantages are:

... some banks are reluctant to deal with the SBA; a few refuse outright.
... there's more paperwork, delays, and red tape, although the process has been greatly streamlined in recent years.
... because of politics, the SBA has unusual responsibilities as a lender.
... many SBA offices are efficient and caring, but this is not true for every office.
... many SBA employees and officers have no direct small business experience; they're career government employees and have not faced the business risks that you are facing.

If everything works properly, all three parties—the bank, the SBA, and you, benefit:

1. The *bank* gets the guarantee of the U.S. government for a majority of the loan. Bankers like to have two ways to get out of a loan (personal guarantees and business assets, for example) and some look for three. The SBA gives them one way out. Also, the bank has an opportunity to make a better profit on the entire transaction. What it does is sell the guaranteed portion of the loan on what is known as the "secondary market," get back most of the principal immediately, and collect a processing fee of a couple of percentage points. The buyer of the guaranteed portion, usually a private individual, receives a U.S. government obligation.
2. The *SBA* fulfills its mission to help small business.
3. *You* get your seed money.

As a startup business, you'll encounter one of four banking situations. The first is the bank that chooses not to work with the SBA for whatever reason. This means you deal only with the bank. If you secure the loan from such a bank, the SBA consideration is immaterial. The primary reason for an SBA guarantee is basically to help the bank; if a bank is willing to work directly with you, there's a lot less paperwork.

The other three banking situations are:

1. The Preferred Lenders Programs.
2. The Certified Lenders Program.
3. A participating bank—one that works with the SBA but doesn't come under either of these two programs.

Let's examine them in reverse order.

Remember that banks aren't the only organizations working with the SBA. Other lending institutions such as commercial finance companies (Commercial Credit Corp., The Money Store) are also authorized by the SBA. So, although I speak of banks, keep in mind that the field is bigger.

Participating Bank

A participating bank will give you the proper SBA forms. Although these change from time to time, they usually include a Personal Financial Statement, a Statement of Personal History, and an Application For Business Loan. Samples of these are shown on the following pages. The forms are then sent to the nearest SBA office for approval by the agency, after you have returned them to the bank. The approval process may take up to 60 days, and if approved, you'll be asked to sign more documents.* One of these is called the Authorization and Loan Agreement which describes the terms of the loan and the collateral offered. It states that you must keep proper financial records, and it limits your ability to pay dividends and bonuses without the written consent of the lender or the SBA.

In addition, the agreement has several documents attached to it, usually including:

1. The SBA note—the actual loan agreement. A 1 percent guarantee fee must be paid to the SBA and it normally is deducted from the loan proceeds.

---

* This is on the high side. A ten-day turnaround is possible in some offices.

Form Approved
OMB No. 100-R-0081

PERSONAL FINANCIAL STATEMENT	Return to:	For SBA Use Only
As of_____ , 19 ___.	Small Business Administration	SBA Loan No.

Complete this form if 1) a sole proprietorship by the proprietor; 2) a partnership by each partner; 3) a corporation by each officer and each stockholder with **20%** or more ownership; 4) any other person or entity providing a guaranty on the loan.

Name and Address, Including ZIP Code   *(of person and spouse submitting Statement)*

SOCIAL SECURITY NO. _____

Business *(of person submitting Statement)*

This statement is submitted in connection with S.B.A. loan requested or granted to the individual or firm, whose name appears below:

Name and Address of Applicant or Borrower, Including ZIP Code

Please answer all questions using "No" or "None" where necessary

ASSETS		LIABILITIES	
Cash on Hand & In Banks . . . . $_____		Accounts Payable. . . . . $_____	
Savings Account in Banks . . . . _____		Notes Payable to Banks . . . . _____	
U. S. Government Bonds . . . . _____		(Describe below - Section 2)	
Accounts & Notes Receivable . . . . _____		Notes Payable to Others . . . . _____	
Life Insurance-Cash Surrender Value Only . . _____		(Describe below - Section 2)	
Other Stocks and Bonds . . . . _____		Installment Account (Auto) . . . . _____	
(Describe - reverse side - Section 3)		Monthly Payments $_____	
Real Estate . . . . _____		Installment Accounts (Other). . . . . _____	
(Describe - reverse side - Section 4)		Monthly Payments $_____	
Automobile - Present Value . . . . _____		Loans on Life Insurance . . . . _____	
Other Personal Property . . . . _____		Mortgages on Real Estate . . . . _____	
(Describe - reverse side - Section 5)		(Describe - reverse side - Section 4)	
Other Assets . . . . _____		Unpaid Taxes. _____	
(Describe - reverse side - Section 6)		(Describe - reverse side - Section 7)	
		Other Liabilities. . . . . _____	
		(Describe - reverse side - Section 8)	
		Total Liabilities. . . . . _____	
		Net Worth . . . . _____	
Total. . . . . $_____		Total. . . . . $_____	

Section I. Source of Income	CONTINGENT LIABILITIES
(Describe below all items listed in this Section)	
Salary. . . . . $_____	As Endorser or Co-Maker . . . . $_____
Net Investment Income. . . . . _____	Legal Claims and Judgments . . . . _____
Real Estate Income. . . . . _____	Provision for Federal Income Tax . . . . _____
Other Income (Describe)* . . . . _____	Other Special Debt . . . . _____

Description of items listed in Section I _____

_____

_____

_____

_____

_____

_____

*Not necessary to disclose alimony or child support payments in "Other Income" unless it is desired to have such payments counted toward total income.

Life Insurance Held (Give face amount of policies - name of company and beneficiaries) _____

_____

_____

_____

_____

_____

_____

_____

_____

_____

SUPPLEMENTARY SCHEDULES

Section 2. Notes Payable to Banks and Others

Name and Address of Holder of Note	Amount of Loan		Terms of Repayments	Maturity of Loan	How Endorsed, Guaranteed, or Secured
	Original Bal.	Present Bal.			
	$	$	$		

Section 3. Other Stocks and Bonds: Give listed and unlisted Stocks and Bonds *(Use separate sheet if necessary)*

No. of Shares	Names of Securities	Cost	Market Value Statement Date	
			Quotation	Amount

Section 4. Real Estate Owned. *(List each parcel separately. Use supplemental sheets if necessary. Each sheet must be identified as a supplement to this statement and signed). (Also advises whether property is covered by title insurance, abstract of title, or both).*

Title is in name of	Type of property

Address of property (City and State)	
	Original Cost to (me) (us) $ _____
	Date Purchased _____
	Present Market Value $ _____
	Tax Assessment Value $ _____

Name and Address of Holder of Mortgage (City and State)	
	Date of Mortgage _____
	Original Amount $ _____
	Balance $ _____
	Maturity _____
	Terms of Payment _____

Status of Mortgage, i.e., current or delinquent. If delinquent describe delinquencies

Section 5. Other Personal Property. *(Describe and if any is mortgaged, state name and address of mortgage holder and amount of mortgage, terms of payment and if delinquent, describe delinquency.)*

Section 6. Other Assets. *(Describe)*

Section 7. Unpaid Taxes. *(Describe in detail, as to type, to whom payable, when due, amount, and what, if any, property a tax lien, if any, attaches)*

Section 8. Other Liabilities. *(Describe in detail)*

(I) or (We) certify the above and the statements contained in the schedules herein is a true and accurate statement of (my) or (our) financial condition as of the date stated herein. This statement is given for the purpose of: *(Check one of the following)*

☐ Inducing S.B.A. to grant a loan as requested in application, of the individual or firm whose name appears herein, in connection with which this statement is submitted.

☐ Furnishing a statement of (my) or (our) financial condition, pursuant to the terms of the guaranty executed by (me) or (us) at the time S.B.A. granted a loan to the individual or firm, whose name appears herein.

Signature	Signature	Date

Return Executed Copies 1, 2, and 3 to SBA

United States of America

SMALL BUSINESS ADMINISTRATION

STATEMENT OF PERSONAL HISTORY

Please Read Carefully - Print or Type

Each member of the small business concern requesting assistance or the development company must submit this form in TRIPLICATE for filing with the SBA application. This form must be filled out and submitted:

1. If a sole proprietorship, by the proprietor;
2. If a partnership, by each partner;
3. If a corporation or a development company, by each officer, director, and additionally, by each holder of 20% or more of the voting stock;
4. Any other person, including a hired manager, who has authority to speak for and commit the borrower in the management of the business.

Name and Address of Applicant (Firm Name)(Street, City, State and ZIP Code)

SBA District Office and City

Amount Applied for:

1. Personal Statement of: (State name in full, if no middle name, state (NMN), or if initial only, indicate initial). List all former names used, and dates each name was used. Use separate sheet if necessary.

First   Middle   Last

2. Date of Birth: (Month, day and year)

3. Place of Birth: (City & State or Foreign Country)

U.S. Citizen? ☐ yes   ☐ no

If no, give alien registration number:
#

4. Give the percentage of ownership or stock owned or to be owned in the small business concern or the Development Company.

Social Security No.

5. Present residence address

From   To   Address

City   State

Home Telephone No. (Include A/C)

Business Telephone No. (Include A/C)

Immediate past residence address

From   To   Address

BE SURE TO ANSWER THE NEXT 3 QUESTIONS CORRECTLY BECAUSE THEY ARE IMPORTANT.

THE FACT THAT YOU HAVE AN ARREST OR CONVICTION RECORD WILL NOT NECESSARILY DISQUALIFY YOU. BUT AN INCORRECT ANSWER WILL PROBABLY CAUSE YOUR APPLICATION TO BE TURNED DOWN.

6. Are you presently under indictment, on parole or probation?

☐ Yes   ☐ No   If yes, furnish details in a separate exhibit. List name(s) under which held, if applicable.

7. Have you ever been charged with or arrested for any criminal offense other than a minor motor vehicle violation?

☐ Yes   ☐ No   If yes, furnish details in a separate exhibit. List name(s) under which charged, if applicable.

8. Have you ever been convicted of any criminal offense other than a minor motor vehicle violation?

☐ Yes   ☐ No   If yes, furnish details in a separate exhibit. List name(s) under which convicted, if applicable.

9. Name and address of participating bank

The information on this form will be used in connection with an investigation of your character. Any information you wish to submit, that you feel will expedite this investigation should be set forth.

Whoever makes any statement knowing it to be false, for the purpose of obtaining for himself or for any applicant, any loan, or loan extension by renewal, deferment or otherwise, or for the purpose of obtaining, or influencing SBA toward, anything of value under the Small Business Act, as amended, shall be punished under Section 16(a) of that Act, by a fine of not more than $5000, or by imprisonment for not more than 2 years, or both.

Signature

Title

Date

It is against SBA's policy to provide assistance to persons not of good character and therefore consideration is given to the qualities and personality traits of a person, favorable and unfavorable, relating thereto, including behavior, integrity, candor and disposition toward criminal actions. It is also against SBA's policy to provide assistance not in the best interests of the United States, for example, if there is reason to believe that the effect of such assistance will be to encourage or support, directly or indirectly, activities inimical to the Security of the United States. Anyone concerned with the collection of this information, as to its voluntariness, disclosure or routine uses may contact the FOIA Office, 1441 "L" Street, N.W., and a copy of §9 "Agency Collection of Information" from SOP 40 04 will be provided.

SBA FORM 912 (3-79) SOP 50 10 1 EDITION OF 5-78 WILL BE USED UNTIL STOCK IS EXHAUSTED

1. SBA FILE COPY

Form Approved
OBM No. 3245-0016

U.S. Small Business Administration

APPLICATION FOR BUSINESS LOAN

I. Applicant

30

Trade Name of Borrower	Street Address
32	34

City	County	State	Zip	Tel. No. (Inc, A/C)
36		37	39	

Employers ID Number	Date of Application	Date Application Received by SBA	Number of Employees (including subsidiaries and affiliates)
33		5	

Type of Business	Date Business Established	☐ Existing Business	At Time of Application _____
		☐ New Business	If Loan is Approved _____
Bank of Business Account		☐ Purchase Existing Business	

II. Management (Proprietor, partners, officers, directors and stockholders owning 20% or more of outstanding stock)

Name	Address	% Owned	Annual Comp.	*Military Service From	*Military Service To	*Race	*Sex
			$				
			$				
			$				
			$				

*This data is collected for statistical purposes only. It has no bearing on the credit decision to approve or decline this application.

III. Use of Proceeds: (Enter Gross Dollar Amounts Rounded to Nearest Hundreds)

	Loan Requested	SBA USE ONLY Approved
5 Land Acquisition	$	
6 New Plant or Building Construction		
7 Building Expansion or Repair		
8 Acquisition and/or Repair of Machinery and Equipment		
9 Inventory Purchase		
10 Working Capital (Including Accounts Payable)		
11 Acquisition of all or part of Existing Business		
12a Payoff SBA Loan		
12b Payoff Bank Loan (Non SBA Associated)		
12c Other Debt Payment (Non SBA Associated)		
13 All Other		
14 Total Loan Requested	$	
Term of Loan		

2 SBA Office Code   1 ① SBA Loan Number

IV. Summary of Collateral:

If your collateral consists of (A) Land and Building, (D) Accounts Receivable and/or (E) Inventory, fill in the appropriate blanks. If you are pledging (B) Machinery and Equipment, (C) Furniture and Fixtures, and/or (F) Other, please provide an itemized list (labeled Exhibit A) that contains serial and identification numbers for all articles that had an original value greater than $500. Include a legal description of Real Estate offered as collateral.

	Present Market Value	Present Mortgage Balance	Cost Less Depreciation
A. Land and Building	$	$	$
B. Machinery & Equipment			
C. Furniture & Fixtures			
D. Accounts Receivable			
E. Inventory			
F. Other			
Total Collateral	$	$	$

V. Previous Government Financing: If you or any principals or affiliates have ever requested Government Financing (including SBA), complete the following:

Name of Agency	Amount	Date of Request	Approved or Declined	Balance	Status
	$			$	
	$			$	
	$			$	

3 Previous SBA Financing (Check One)
☐ (1) No   ☐ (2) Repaid/Other   ☐ (3) Present Borrower

4 Loan Number of 1st SBA Loan

VI. Indebtedness: Furnish the following information on all installment debts, contracts, notes, and mortgages payable. Indicate by an asterisk (*) items to be paid by loan proceeds and reason for paying same (present balance should agree with latest balance sheet submitted).

To Whom Payable	Original Amount	Original Date	Present Balance	Rate of Interest	Maturity Date	Monthly Payment	Security	Current or Delinquent
	$		$			$		
	$		$			$		
	$		$			$		
	$		$			$		

SBA Form 4 (9-81) REF SOP 50 10 1   PREVIOUS EDITIONS ARE OBSOLETE   (OVER)

All Exhibits must be signed and dated by person signing this form.

1. Submit SBA Form 912 (Personal History Statement) for each person e.g. owners, partners, directors, major stockholders, etc; the instructions are on SBA Form 912.

2. Furnish a signed current personal balance sheet (SBA Form 413 may be used for this purpose) for each stockholder (with 20% or greater ownership), partner, officer, and owner. Social Security number should be included on personal financial statement. Label this Exhibit B.

3. Include the statements listed below: 1, 2, 3 for the last three years; also 1, 2, 3, 4 dated within 90 days of filing the application; and statement 5, if applicable. This is Exhibit C (SBA has Management Aids that help in the preparation of financial statements.)

    1. Balance Sheet   2. Profit and Loss Statement
    3. Reconciliation of Net Worth
    4. Aging of Accounts Receivable and Payable
    5. Earnings projections for at least one year where financial statements for the last three years are unavailable or where requested by District Office.

       (If Profit and Loss Statement is not available, explain why and substitute Federal Income Tax Forms.)

4. Provide a brief history of your company and a paragraph describing the expected benefits it will receive from the loan. Label it Exhibit D.

5. Provide a brief description of the educational, technical and business background for all the people listed in Section II under Management. Please mark it Exhibit E.

6. Do you have any co-signers and/or guarantors for this loan? If so, please submit their names, addresses and personal balance sheet(s) as Exhibit F.

7. Are you buying machinery or equipment with your loan money? If so, you must include a list of the equipment and the cost. This is Exhibit G.

8. Have you or any officers of your company ever been involved in bankruptcy or insolvency proceedings? If so, please provide the details as Exhibit H. If none, check here ☐

9. Are you or your business involved in any pending lawsuits? If yes, provide the details as Exhibit I. If none, check here ☐

10. Do you or your spouse or any member of your household, or anyone who owns, manages, or directs your business or their spouses or members of their households work for the Small Business Administration, Small Business Advisory Council, SCORE or ACE, any Federal Agency, or the participating lender? If so, please provide the name and address of the person and the office where employed. Label this Exhibit J. If none, check here ☐

11. Does your business have any subsidiaries or affiliates? If yes, please provide their names and the relationship with your company along with a current balance sheet and operating statement for each. This should be Exhibit K.

12. Do you buy from, sell to, or use the services of any concern in which someone in your company has a significant financial interest? If yes, provide details on a separate sheet of paper labeled Exhibit L.

13. If your business is a franchise, include a copy of the franchise agreement and a copy of the FTC disclosure statement supplied to you by the Franchisor. Please include it as Exhibit M.

CONSTRUCTION LOANS ONLY

14. Include in a separate exhibit (Exhibit N) the estimated cost of the project and a statement of the source of any additional funds.

15. File all the necessary compliance documents (SBA Form Series 601). The loan officer will advise which forms are necessary.

16. Provide copies of preliminary construction plans and specifications. Include them as Exhibit O. Final plans will be required prior to disbursement.

DIRECT LOANS ONLY

17. Include two bank declination letters with your application. These letters should include the name and telephone number of the persons contacted at the banks, the amount and terms of the loan, the reason for decline and whether or not the bank will participate with SBA. In cities with 200,000 people or less, one letter will be sufficient.

AGREEMENTS AND CERTIFICATIONS

Agreement of Nonemployment of SBA Personnel: I/We agree that if SBA approves this loan application I/We will not, for at least two years, hire as an employee or consultant anyone that was employed by the SBA during the one year period prior to the disbursement of the loan.

Certification: I/We certify: (a) I/We have not paid anyone connected with the Federal Government for help in getting this loan. I/We also agree to report to the SBA Office of Security and Investigations, 1441 L Street N.W., Washington, D.C., 20416 any Federal Government employee who offers, in return for any type of compensation, to help get this loan approved.

(b) All information in this application and the Exhibits is true and complete to the best of my/our knowledge and is submitted to SBA so SBA can decide whether to grant a loan or participate with a lending institution in a loan to me/us. I/We agree to pay for or reimburse SBA for the cost of any surveys, title or mortgage examinations, appraisals etc., performed by non-SBA personnel provided I/We have given my/our consent.

(c) I/We give the assurance that we will comply with sections 112 and 113 of Title 13 of the Code of Federal Regulations. These Code sections prohibit discrimination on the grounds of race, color, sex, religion, marital status, handicap, age, or national origin by recipients of Federal financial assistance and require appropriate reports and access to books and records. These requirements are applicable to anyone who buys or takes control of the business. I/We realize that if I/We do not comply with these non-discrimination requirements SBA can call, terminate, or accelerate repayment of my/our loan. As consideration for any Management and Technical Assistance that may be provided, I/We waive all claims against SBA and its consultants.

I/We understand that I/We need not pay anybody to deal with SBA. I/We have read and understand Form 394 which explains SBA policy on representatives and their fees.

For Guaranty Loans please provide an original and one copy (Photocopy is Acceptable) of the Application Form, and all Exhibits to the participating lender. For Direct Loans submit one original copy of application and Exhibits to SBA.

It is against SBA regulations to charge the applicant a percentage of the loan proceeds as a fee for preparing this application.

If you make a statement that you know to be false or if you over value a security in order to help obtain a loan under the provisions of the Small Business Act, you can be fined up to $5,000 or be put in jail for up to two years, or both.

_____
Signature of Preparer if Other Than Applicant

_____
Print or Type Name of Preparer

_____
Address of Preparer

If Applicant is a proprietor or general partner, sign below:

By:_____
                                      Date

If Applicant is a corporation, sign below:

Corporate Seal   Date

By:_____
              Signature of President

Attested by: _____
              Signature of Corporate Secretary

2. SBA Settlement Sheet—a form which summarizes the actual disbursement of cash by the bank.

3. Compensation Agreement (see next page for sample). If anyone—accountant, lawyer, consultant—charges you money in connection with the SBA application, you must report it.

Under the CLP, specific individuals at lending institutions are certified by the SBA to complete the proper forms and do the proper investigations, a process taking 10 to 30 days. All the paperwork is then sent to the SBA, which makes sure the forms have been completed properly. The SBA has been shooting for a three-day turnaround for this paperwork.

Certified Lenders' Program (CLP)

Certain banks—Chase Manhattan, for example—make many commercial loans, a majority of them with SBA participation. The SBA authorizes several of these very large institutions to do the entire job themselves, *including* the SBA's part. This program is presently in a test phase and will probably expand to include more banks in the future.

Preferred Lenders' Program (PLP)

Remember again, you don't have to use the SBA. If you can get your bank loan without them, you're better off in the long run because the SBA won't save you either time or money. You'll spend more of both using them. However, if your banker recommends SBA participation, heed that advice. If you and your banker decide on SBA participation, have patience with the procedure. Even if you're asked to do what you feel are silly things, remember what's at stake—your seed money and your business.

Summary

SBA LOAN NO.  _____

COMPENSATION AGREEMENT FOR SERVICES IN CONNECTION WITH

APPLICATION AND LOAN FROM (OR IN PARTICIPATION WITH)

SMALL BUSINESS ADMINISTRATION

This undersigned representative (attorney, accountant, engineer, appraiser, etc.) hereby agrees that the undersigned has not and will not, directly or indirectly, charge or receive any payment in connection with the application for or the making of the loan except for services actually performed on behalf of the Applicant. The undersigned further agrees that the amount of payment for such services shall not exceed an amount deemed reasonable by SBA (and, if it is a participation loan, by the participating lending institution), and to refund any amount in excess of that deemed reasonable by SBA (and the participating institution). This agreement shall supersede any other agreement covering payment for such services.

A general description of the services performed, or to be performed, by the undersigned and the compensation paid or to be paid are set forth below. If the total compensation in any case exceeds $300 (or $50 for: (1) regular business loans of $15,000 or less; (2) all disaster home loans; or (3) all economic opportunity loans), or if SBA should otherwise require, the services must be itemized showing each date services were performed, time spent each day, and description of the service rendered on each day listed. If necessary, the statement of services may be continued on the reverse side of this form, or attached as a rider hereto.

The undersigned Applicant and representative hereby certify that no other fees have been charged or will be charged by the representative in connection with this loan, unless provided for in loan authorization specifically approved by SBA.

DESCRIPTION OF SERVICES

Amount Heretofore Paid $ _____

Additional Amount to be Paid $ _____

Total Compensation $ _____

(Parts 103, 104, and 122 of Title 13 of the Code of Federal Regulations contain provisions covering appearances and compensation of persons representing SBA applicants. Section 103.13-5 authorizes the suspension or revocation of the privilege of any such person to appear before SBA for charging a fee deemed unreasonable by SBA for the services actually performed, charging of unreasonable expenses, or violation of this agreement. In addition, whoever commits any fraud, by false or misleading statement or representation, or by conspiracy. shall be subject to the penalty of any applicable Federal or State statute.)

Dated _____ , 19 ____

_____
(Representative)

By _____

The Applicant hereby certifies to SBA that the above representations, description of services and amounts are correct and satisfactory to Applicant.

Dated _____ , 19 ____

_____
(Applicant)

By _____

The participating lending insitution hereby certifies that the above representations of service rendered and amounts charged are reasonable and satisfactory to said lender.

Dated _____ , 19 ____

_____
(Lender)

By _____

NOTE: Foregoing certificate must be executed, if by a corporation, in corporate name by duly authorized officer and duly attested; if by a partnership, in the firm name, together with signature of a general partner.

**SBA REVIEW BY_____ TITLE_____ DATE_____

SBA FORM 159 (10-74) REF SOP 20 50 PREVIOUS EDITIONS ARE OBSOLETE.

WHITE TO SBA, YELLOW TO BORROWER, PINK TO BORROWER'S REPRESENTATIVE

Other Financing Sources

I said earlier that most small business startups are funded by the entrepreneur, a bank, and a few investors who are usually friends and relatives. Although there are no statistics available, I estimate that 90 to 95 percent of the businesses get going this way. The remaining 5 to 10 percent use other sources. What's surprising is the number of sources available. I'm going to cover some of the more common ones, but remember to be on the lookout for others that may be of use to you.

Commercial Finance Companies

You can find these institutions in the Yellow Pages under "Loans." Basically, a commercial finance company works with you just the way a bank does; they want the same documentation and collateral. Some of them are also approved SBA lending institutions under the CLP. Because finance companies are not regulated in the same way banks are, they can legally take more risk. Their default ratio on their amount of outstanding loans is higher, and therefore, the interest rates they charge may be greater. Many aren't very professional in their dealings with small business. When you see an ex-baseball player advertising "no limit loans" and "money for any worthwhile purpose," you should wonder. The other problem with a finance company is that you're only a borrower to them. If you have a loan from a commercial bank and keep your business and personal accounts there, you're a total customer of that bank. If you run into a financial snag, your banker is going to be more flexible than a finance company will be.

State and Local Development Authorities

Every state and practically every city with a population greater than 10,000 has a development authority. State agencies, usually called economic development departments, won't be of much help to you as a startup because they're more interested in larger projects. However, your local authority may be of assistance, especially if you're starting a venture employing more than one or two people. If the local authority doesn't provide startup financing, they may know of some group that does. A book that lists all state agencies as well as many other valuable sources is *The Insider's Guide to Small Business Resources* by David E. Gumpert and Jeffry A. Timmons (1982, Doubleday & Co., Garden City, NY).

99

Venture Capital   If cousin Louie throws a few grand into your startup, he's technically a venture capitalist—or adventure capitalist if you prefer. Chances are, though, that Louie isn't very sophisticated when it comes to business finance and is only doing it to help you. Other than the Louies of the world, true venture capitalists come in four flavors.

Before I briefly discuss these types of investors, let me give you some general background. Cousin Louie is putting money into your company because he likes you and wants you to succeed. Venture capitalists (sometimes called vulture capitalists) have one goal and one goal only—money. They will invest in a business if they believe the management team has a good idea and can cause the venture to grow very rapidly and reach significant size in a short period of time. How large is "significant size" and how long is a "short period?" This varies, but if you cannot show that your company will reach several million dollars in annual sales in five years, not too many venture capitalists will be interested in talking with you.

How do they work? In most instances, a venture capitalist will make an equity investment in your business, thus obtaining some degree of ownership. Therefore, you will sell a percentage of the company and this can vary from 20 percent to 70 percent depending on the circumstances. Some entrepreneurs believe that they should always keep more than 50 percent of the business, in order to retain control. This is not a hard and fast rule and there are two considerations. First, if venture financing is what you need to propel your startup to a sizable business, owning 20 percent of an elephant may be preferable to 100 percent of a mouse (and sometimes a dead one at that). In the second place, sophisticated investors like venture capitalists realize that if they leave the entrepreneur with little of his or her company, the entrepreneur may lose interest in the business. The investment-ownership balance is, of course, negotiable.

At some future time, the venture capitalist wants to "convert," meaning selling his ownership for a lot more than he paid for it. This sale could be to you, to another investor, or to the general public, as in the case with a stock offering. To get to that stage, the business must grow and be profitable, so there will be constant pressure on you to do this. The venture capitalist will certainly demand a position on your board of directors, which can have both an advantage (you will get good, professional counsel) as well as a disadvantage (you may wind up with a "boss").

Here, then, are the four kinds of venture capitalists:

1. *Private individuals,* who make equity investments in small businesses, can't be found in any directory. They keep a low profile but are often known to bankers, accountants, insurance agents, and stockbrokers. Let one of these people make the introductions and try to have the potential investor come to you. Before you sit down with someone like this, be certain you know how much of the company you're willing to give up (sell) for what kind of money. There are a few sharpies out there who may try to get 70 to 90 percent of your company for next to nothing. Some of these folks may want to invest *and* become part of your business; there's nothing wrong with this as long as you feel right about it and the investor has practical business skills. You don't want a bumbler or a meddler, especially one who's a stockholder. Private individuals invest in a range from a few thousand dollars to several hundred thousand.

2. *Private firms,* whose number averages about 300, make average investments of three-quarters of a million. They weed out about 98 percent of

the business proposals, with nine-tenths culled out in the first day. Also, they're looking for companies that can grow to significant size in a relatively short time.

3. *Corporations,* looking for new subsidiaries, number less than 50 in the country; they want almost total ownership and make investments in the millions.
4. *SBICs* or Small Business Investment Companies, of which there are probably 400 at present, are private companies who borrow money from the SBA to supplement their own funds. About 70 percent of these firms only do lending because of the commitment to repay their loans to the government. Your nearest SBA office can give you names of SBICs in your locale. There are also about 100 MESBICs (Minority Enterprise Small Business Investment Companies) who help minority-owned businesses. Both tend to avoid startups.

Unless you have the next Xerox on your hands, you will probably deal only with the first category, private individuals. If you want the most recent list of private venture capital firms, contact *Venture* magazine—35 West 45th Street, New York, NY 10036. They do an annual survey and publish a directory.

Farmer's Home Administration (FmHA)

There are 1,750 rural counties in the United States having FmHA offices. Through their Business and Industry Loan Program, the FmHA guarantees bank loans much like the SBA but with a few differences:

1. Priorities are given to truly rural businesses.
2. The major test used by FmHA is whether the business provides real benefits to the community where the business is located. These benefits include more jobs and/or attracting money from outside the community—tourism, for example.

If you plan to locate in a rural area, check your phone book listing under "U.S. Government—Agriculture Department." Because FmHA's ground rules change from time to time, it's a good idea to call before visiting them.

Customers

If your venture is perceived as a "good business" by your customers, they might want to invest. Another method of financing is to have customers pay in advance; however, this must be handled carefully and judiciously.

Suppliers

Again, they may want to invest, but more common is the use of trade credit. You may find some suppliers willing to extend credit for 30 days and even longer, but it's more likely you'll have to pay cash for your first orders. If you don't ask though, you'll never know.

Employees

If you're going to sell stock to employees, be sure to check with your lawyer first. You may unwittingly create an ESOP—Employee Stock Option Plan—and that has legal ramifications. If you simply plan to borrow money from them, the loan is a standard business loan.

Miscellaneous Sources

Some rather interesting sources can be found if you look around. In a town in Vermont, a fund was established in the will of a wealthy couple to help women who wanted to work on their own as seamstresses. Small foundations exist to give financial aid to people starting in business, and many of these are restricted to people of a particular ethnic group or geography or even place of birth. Take the time to do some asking around. Also contact the professional trade association which serves your industry.

Other sources to consider are:

> . . . local stock investment clubs;
> . . . credit unions;
> . . . savings and loan associations;
> . . . college endowment funds;
> . . . charitable trusts;
> . . . tax-exempt foundations;
> . . . large employers in your town.

Ultimately, of course, the most important source of financing for your business is the profit it produces.

Once You Are Underway

You don't really need the information in this section until your venture has been in existence for several months and, in that respect, this epilogue is not a part of the seed money process. I think it's important, though, or I would not have included it in the book. Seed money helps to establish a business but it will not guarantee success. After its inception, you must give constant attention to your business and what it is doing.

Earlier in the book I compared starting a business and starting a car; both must eventually run on their own or neither gets anywhere. If you accept this methodology, you recognize that when it's constantly applied it goes a long way toward helping your business grow and flourish. I don't want to see you use all the proper methods of obtaining seed money only to abandon the entire methodology once you're underway. If you blow it later, you'll not only lose your own investment, you'll have to pay back the business loan and probably some stockholders as well. If a banker grants you a loan, that man or woman believes the business will make it. For example, if the bank has a commercial loan default rate of, say, 2 percent, your banker gives you *at least* a 98 percent probability of survival.

There are, of course, many things you need to do to monitor your business and keep it healthy. I won't go into all of them here, but I do want to mention a few.

Using Your Business Plan

If you did your plan properly, you have a road map of where you want to go. As in using any map, it's important to check your progress as you go along. If you don't you may get lost and never know it. One of the more important features of your plan is the cash flow projection. It becomes your budget for future months, and when a month passes and your expenses in certain categories are past history, you need to analyze what happened.

Let's start simply. Suppose for March you estimated your telephone expense would be $200 but your bill was actually $300. You might get mad about this, but that won't change the reality of the bill which is $100 higher than you expected. That $100 is called a *variance*. I (unlike accountants) like to write it with parentheses around it to signify a *negative* variance: $(100). It's not only a *dollar* variance, it's also a *percentage* variance:

$$\frac{\$100}{\$200} \times 100 = 50\%$$

or, using our convention, (50%). Notice that to arrive at the percentage variance, we use the budgeted value of $200 for the denominator.

Now, if we want to put all this together in a way that can be easily seen:

Item	Budget	Actual	Dollar Variance	Percent Variance
Telephone	$200	$300	$(100)	(50)

If you analyze all your expenses for a particular month (as you do for the cumulative year-to-date expenses), the variance columns help pinpoint areas for further analysis. With the telephone example, it cost you $100 more than you expected. The question is: why? Did you make more long-distance calls than you planned? Were these calls legitimate? Do you have a tendency to talk too long? Possibly your budgets for telephone expense in the months to come should be increased. The important point here is that variance analysis gives you information to make future decisions.

Let's do a more complex example with several budget items. Consider the information below. The columns under Year-to-Date represent totals for January, February, and March. Notice that although the total March expenses came in $160, or 14 percent, over budget, the same year-to-date figure shows the business under budget by $100, or 3 percent.

The question often asked is, "Should I analyze every item?" Probably not, but you should have some kind of decision-making rule. For example, our hypothetical business owner may decide that she'll examine any item whose monthly variance is more than 50 percent or $100, whichever is greater. In our example, she investigates the reasons behind the variances in telephone, advertising, delivery expense, and office supplies. She doesn't bother with utilities because the dollar amount, $10, is less than $100 and the percent variance, 11 percent, is under 50 percent. I suggest you analyze both overages *and* underages. Just because an expense is lower than you planned does not make it "good." It may mean you're not spending the money you should in those areas.

The next page is a blank form for you to use. Simply make 12 copies for a year's analysis.

Analyzing Performance

It's absolutely appalling to me the number of business owners who don't bother to see what their financial information is telling them. They prepare financial statements or have their accountant do it; they give the statements a quick look to see if they made a profit, then heave them into the bottom desk

XYZ BUSINESS
Month of March 19xx

Item	Current Month				Year-to-Date			
	Budget	Actual	Dollar Variance	Percent Variance	Budget	Actual	Dollar Variance	Percent Variance
Telephone	$ 200	$ 300	$(100)	(50)	$ 700	$ 900	$(200)	(29)
Utilities	90	80	10	11	300	250	50	17
Advertising	620	760	(140)	(23)	2100	1930	170	8
Delivery Exp.	40	60	(20)	(50)	120	120	—	—
Office Supplies	170	80	90	53	380	300	80	21
Totals	$1120	$1280	$(160)	(14)	$3600	$3500	$100	3

Name of Business:

Month:

	Current Month				Year-to-Date			
Item	Budget	Actual	Dollar Variance	Percent Variance	Budget	Actual	Dollar Variance	Percent Variance
1.								
2.								
3.								
4.								
5.								
6.								
7.								
8.								
9.								
10.								
11.								
12.								
13.								
14.								
15.								
16.								
17.								
18.								
19.								
20.								
TOTALS								

drawer. Analyze these statements so you know what's going on. Also send these statements to your banker with *your* analysis attached.

What's the best way to analyze the income statement and the balance sheet? Use the financial ratios published by Robert Morris Associates (*Annual Statement Studies,* referenced earlier) or other annually published sources:

1. National Cash Register's *Expenses in Retail Business*
   write to: NCR Corp., Dayton, OH 45479.

2. Dun & Bradstreet's *Cost of Doing Business*
   write to: Dun & Bradstreet, 99 Church Street, New York, NY 10007.

3. *Almanac of Business and Financial Ratios* by Leo Troy (Prentice-Hall, Englewood Cliffs, NJ).

I like the RMA material and will use their sample for SIC 5621 (women's ready-to-wear apparel) for our example. Consider the financial statements for Lady Lenore, a women's clothing store, on page 107, as well as the page from the RMA book (pages 108 and 109) and their standard disclaimers (below).

Interpretation of Statement Studies Figures

RMA recommends that Statement Studies data be regarded only as general guidelines and not as absolute industry norms. There are several reasons why the data may not be fully representative of a given industry:

(1) The financial statements used in the *Statement Studies* are not selected by any random or statistically reliable method. RMA member banks voluntarily submit the raw data they have available each year, with these being the only constraints: (a) The fiscal year-ends of the companies reported may not be from April 1 through June 29, and (b) their total assets must be less than $100 million.

(2) Many companies have varied product lines; however, the *Statement Studies* categorize them by their primary product Standard Industrial Classification (SIC) number only.

(3) Some of our industry samples are rather small in relation to the total number of firms in a given industry. A relatively small sample can increase the chances that some of our composites do not fully represent an industry.

(4) There is the chance that an extreme statement can be present in a sample, causing a disproportionate influence on the industry composite. This is particularly true in a relatively small sample.

(5) Companies within the same industry may differ in their method of operations which in turn can directly influence their financial statements. Since they are included in our sample, too, these statements can significantly affect our composite calculations.

(6) Other considerations that can result in variations among different companies engaged in the same general line of business are different labor markets; geographical location; different accounting methods; quality of products handled; sources and methods of financing; and terms of sale.

For these reasons, RMA does not recommend the Statement Studies *figures be considered as absolute norms for a given industry. Rather the figures should be used only as general guidelines and in addition to the other methods of financial analysis. RMA makes no claim as to the representativeness of the figures printed in this book.*

As I said before, I'm not going to teach you the basics of business accounting. If you don't understand income statements and balance sheets, additional reading or course work is critical to the survival of your business.

Reading the RMA sheet takes a little doing. First of all, we want the column on the far left because it's for businesses with asset size 0-1MM, zero to one million dollars, and Lady Lenore is in that category. Notice that the first three blocks are percentages—one for assets, one for liabilities, one for items on the income statement.

Let's start with the very first item—cash. The RMA data shows that the average cash held by the 242 retailers surveyed is 10.1% of total assets. For Lady Lenore, the percentage of cash to total assets is

INCOME STATEMENT
LADY LENORE, INC.
for the fiscal year ended June 30, 19xx

			Percent
Net Sales		$300,000	100.0
Cost of Sales		188,000	62.7
Gross Profit		$112,000	37.3
Expenses:			
Payroll expense	$38,700		12.9
Office supplies	1,800		0.6
Advertising	7,200		2.4
Insurance	2,000		0.7
Taxes and fees	1,200		0.4
Travel & entertainment	1,700		0.5
Dues & subscriptions	300		0.1
Telephone	2,800		0.9
Utilities	1,600		0.5
Rent	14,400		4.8
Interest	8,400		2.8
Depreciation	3,000		1.0
Owner's salary	19,500		6.5
Miscellaneous	1,500		0.5
Total Expenses		104,100	34.6
Profit Before Tax		$ 7,900	2.7
Federal and State Taxes		1,200	0.4
Profit After Tax		$ 6,700	2.3

BALANCE SHEET
Lady Lenore, Inc. as of June 30, 19xx

Current Assets		Current Liabilities	
Cash	$ 4,200	Notes Payable	$ 8,500
Accounts Receivable	33,700	Current Portion, LTD	9,100
Inventory	72,000	Accounts Payable	29,000
Other C/A	9,100	Accrued Expenses	3,700
		Other Payables	1,300
Total Current Assets	$119,000	Total Current Liabilities	$ 51,600
Fixed Assets		Long-Term Debt	61,000
(net of depreciation)	27,000	Total Liabilities	$112,600
Other Assets	8,200	NET WORTH	
		Owner's Equity	$ 33,000
		Retained Earnings	8,600
		Total Net Worth	$ 41,600
TOTAL ASSETS	$154,200	LIABILITIES + NET WORTH	$154,200

RETAILERS - WOMEN'S READY-TO-WEAR
SIC# 5621

251

	Current Data					Comparative Historical Data				
	171(6/30-9/30/82)		178(10/1/82-3/31/83)			6/30/78-3/31/79	6/30/79-3/31/80	6/30/80-3/31/81	6/30/81-3/31/82	6/30/82-3/31/83
ASSET SIZE	0-1MM	1-10MM	10-50MM	50-100MM	ALL	ALL	ALL	ALL	ALL	ALL
NUMBER OF STATEMENTS	242	86	17	4	349	296	337	334	323	349
ASSETS	%	%	%	%	%	%	%	%	%	%
Cash & Equivalents	10.1	10.5	8.3		10.1	12.6	12.0	11.1	10.9	10.1
Accts. & Notes Rec. - Trade(net)	14.5	19.5	19.3		16.1	17.6	17.5	17.0	16.3	16.1
Inventory	51.8	40.8	37.0		48.1	44.0	44.3	45.7	47.5	48.1
All Other Current	1.6	1.6	5.4		1.8	2.2	2.1	1.2	1.4	1.8
Total Current	78.0	72.4	70.0		76.1	76.4	75.9	75.1	76.0	76.1
Fixed Assets (net)	15.7	20.1	23.3		17.4	16.6	17.1	17.9	18.0	17.4
Intangibles (net)	1.3	.9	1.1		1.1	.9	.8	.6	.7	1.1
All Other Non-Current	5.1	6.6	5.5		5.4	6.1	6.2	6.4	5.2	5.4
Total	100.0	100.0	100.0		100.0	100.0	100.0	100.0	100.0	100.0
LIABILITIES										
Notes Payable-Short Term	8.7	7.9	3.2		8.2	8.5	9.4	8.4	9.0	8.2
Cur. Mat-L/T/D	3.5	3.0	1.7		3.2	2.5	3.1	3.1	3.4	3.2
Accts. & Notes Payable - Trade	17.1	24.3	18.5		19.0	19.6	19.1	19.1	19.5	19.0
Accrued Expenses	4.9	6.8	9.6		5.6	6.6	5.8	6.0	5.8	5.6
All Other Current	3.1	3.5	1.6		3.1	3.1	3.4	3.1	3.0	3.1
Total Current	37.3	45.5	34.6		39.1	40.2	40.7	39.6	40.6	39.1
Long Term Debt	15.7	12.7	10.1		14.8	13.8	12.8	12.8	15.1	14.8
All Other Non-Current	2.9	1.9	4.3		2.8	1.4	1.7	2.1	1.9	2.8
Net Worth	44.1	39.9	51.0		43.4	44.6	44.8	45.5	42.4	43.4
Total Liabilities & Net Worth	100.0	100.0	100.0		100.0	100.0	100.0	100.0	100.0	100.0
INCOME DATA										
Net Sales	100.0	100.0	100.0		100.0	100.0	100.0	100.0	100.0	100.0
Cost Of Sales	59.8	61.1	64.3		60.5	58.7	59.2	59.1	59.5	60.5
Gross Profit	40.2	38.9	35.7		39.5	41.3	40.8	40.9	40.5	39.5
Operating Expenses	37.4	37.8	31.3		37.0	38.3	38.1	38.4	37.4	37.0
Operating Profit	2.9	1.1	4.3		2.5	3.0	2.7	2.6	3.2	2.5
All Other Expenses (net)	.5	-.4	.0		.3	-.2	.0	.0	.7	.3
Profit Before Taxes	2.4	1.5	4.3		2.3	3.3	2.7	2.6	2.5	2.3
RATIOS										
Current	3.4	2.3	2.5		3.2	2.9	2.8	2.9	2.9	3.2
	2.3	1.6	2.1		2.1	1.9	2.0	2.0	2.0	2.1
	1.5	1.2	1.7		1.5	1.5	1.5	1.5	1.4	1.5
Quick	1.1	1.0	1.2		1.2	1.2	1.2	1.2	1.2	1.2
	.7	.7	.9		.7	.8	.7	.7	.7	.7
	.3	.3	.2		.3	.4	.4	.4	.3	.3
	(241)		(348)		(348)	(295)	(333)	(322)	(348)	(348)
Sales/Receivables	2 190.4	5 80.7	2 197.3		2 159.0	5 77.6	5 80.3	3 110.5	3 110.5	2 159.0
	13 27.1	21 17.2	34 10.7		15 24.3	20 18.7	19 18.0	17 21.8	17 21.8	15 24.3
	38 9.7	54 6.8	51 7.1		42 8.6	46 8.0	46 8.0	41 9.0	41 9.0	42 8.6

81	4.5	**65**	5.6	**61**	6.0		**74**	4.9	Cost of Sales/Inventory	**74**	4.9	**72**	5.1	**74**	4.9	**73**	5.0	**74**	4.9
114	3.2	**89**	4.1	**76**	4.8		**104**	3.5		**101**	3.6	**94**	3.9	**104**	3.5	**107**	3.4	**104**	3.5
166	2.2	**114**	3.2	**111**	3.3		**152**	2.4		**146**	2.5	**135**	2.7	**152**	2.4	**152**	2.4	**152**	2.4
	4.2		5.5		4.9			4.5	Sales/Working Capital		4.6		4.8		4.6		4.6		4.5
	6.3		10.3		6.3			7.0			6.7		7.0		6.7		7.3		7.0
	10.4		21.7		9.7			12.3			12.1		12.7		14.8		13.8		12.3
	5.0		6.4		7.1			5.4	EBIT/Interest		8.9		7.2		6.0		5.1		5.4
(203)	2.0	(73)	2.0	(12)	2.8		(290)	2.0		(246)	4.0	(268)	3.3	(260)	2.4	(264)	2.4	(290)	2.0
	1.1		.9		1.4			1.0			1.6		1.3		.9		1.1		1.0
	5.1		4.6		12.7			6.0	Cash Flow/Cur. Mat. L/T/D		5.7		4.3		5.4		5.4		6.0
(71)	2.1	(52)	1.9	(11)	7.6		(137)	2.2		(114)	2.0	(133)	1.9	(134)	2.2	(129)	2.5	(137)	2.2
	.7		.8		2.2			.9			1.0		.8		.7		.8		.9
	.1		.3		.2			.2	Fixed/Worth		.2		.2		.2		.2		.2
	.3		.5		.4			.4			.3		.3		.4		.4		.4
	.7		.9		.7			.8			.6		.7		.7		.7		.8
	.6		.8		.6			.6	Debt/Worth		.7		.6		.6		.7		.6
	1.2		1.7		.8			1.3			1.2		1.2		1.2		1.4		1.3
	2.5		2.6		1.5			2.5			2.3		2.3		2.2		2.6		2.5
	32.2		28.6		33.8			30.6	% Profit Before Taxes/Tangible Net Worth		32.8		30.3		26.5		29.7		30.6
(227)	12.5	(84)	9.2		20.5		(332)	12.2		(285)	14.8	(326)	15.7	(326)	13.3	(306)	14.4	(332)	12.2
	1.7		.4		7.4			1.8			7.1		4.7		1.5		2.6		1.8
	13.0		10.9		18.3			12.6	% Profit Before Taxes/Total Assets		12.8		13.7		12.5		12.6		12.6
	5.3		4.0		9.2			4.9			6.6		6.3		5.6		5.8		4.9
	.4		.1		3.6			.4			2.5		1.4		.2		.6		.4
	47.9		24.3		22.6			42.9	Sales/Net Fixed Assets		38.0		37.2		35.2		36.1		42.9
	24.2		14.2		12.9			19.9			18.9		19.3		17.5		18.8		19.9
	13.4		9.6		7.3			10.9			11.2		10.9		10.5		10.1		10.9
	3.3		3.3		2.8			3.3	Sales/Total Assets		3.1		3.3		3.2		3.2		3.3
	2.6		2.6		2.5			2.6			2.5		2.6		2.5		2.6		2.6
	2.0		2.0		2.1			2.0			2.0		2.0		2.0		2.0		2.0
	.8		.8		.9			.8	% Depr., Dep., Amort./Sales		.8		.7		.8		.8		.8
(207)	1.2	(80)	1.4	(15)	1.6		(305)	1.3		(270)	1.1	(294)	1.2	(294)	1.2	(290)	1.2	(305)	1.3
	1.8		1.9		2.5			1.8			1.6		1.7		1.8		1.7		1.8
	3.2		3.6		4.1			3.3	% Lease & Rental Exp/Sales		3.2		3.0		3.1		3.3		3.3
(182)	4.7	(55)	5.3	(11)	5.1		(250)	4.9		(239)	4.9	(247)	4.9	(243)	4.8	(242)	4.8	(250)	4.9
	6.7		6.4		6.2			6.6			6.1		6.1		6.2		6.2		6.6
	3.0		1.5					2.4	% Officers' Comp/Sales		3.0		3.0		2.9		2.7		2.4
(117)	5.0	(34)	2.4				(152)	3.8		(169)	4.8	(171)	5.1	(162)	4.6	(165)	4.8	(152)	3.8
	7.6		3.5					6.6			8.1		7.8		7.4		8.0		6.6
	227797M		709909M		940592M	457483M		2335781M	Net Sales ($)		1252336M		1564064M		1858191M		1719478M		2335781M
	85044M		257786M		387814M	261546M		992190M	Total Assets ($)		524590M		604409M		785492M		707747M		992190M

M = $thousand   MM = $million
See Pages 1 through 12 for Explanation of Ratios and Data

$$\frac{\$4,200}{\$154,200} \times 100 = 2.7\%$$

This is extremely unfavorable. If Lady Lenore were operating at the average level, it would have cash of

$$10.1\% \times \$154,200 = \$15,574$$

Now averages can be misleading, of course, but Lady Lenore is simply too lean. Next is accounts receivable. The RMA average is 14.5%, whereas our store is

$$\frac{\$33,700}{\$154,200} \times 100 = 21.9\%$$

A bit high. If our business owner were to collect some of her receivables and turn them into cash, the business would be more in balance.

The other asset comparisons are listed below:

Item	RMA Value (%)	Lady Lenore (%)
Inventory	51.8	46.7
All Other Current	1.6	5.9
Total Current	78.0	77.1
Fixed Assets (net)	15.7	17.5
Intangibles (net)	1.3	—
All Other Non-Current	5.1	5.3

Things look pretty much in line, with the exception of All Other Current Assets; these are often pre-paid items such as deposits, insurance premiums, or advances.

Now let's do the same for all the liabilities:

Item	RMA Value (%)	Lady Lenore (%)
Notes Payable	8.7	5.5
Current Portion, LTD	3.5	5.9
Accounts Payable	17.1	18.8
Accrued Expenses	4.9	2.4
Other Current	3.1	.8
Total Current	37.3	33.5
Long Term Debt	15.7	39.6
All Other Non-Current	2.9	—
Net Worth	44.1	27.0

Note that items are not always called the same things by different people. We notice three things: current liabilities are slightly low but long term debt is much too high and net worth way too low. Lady Lenore would never be able to raise debt capital with this structure. If she needs funds, she'll have to find an investor or two.

Now let's look at income data the same way:

Item	RMA Value (%)	Lady Lenore (%)
Net Sales	100.0	100.0
Cost of Sales	59.8	62.7
Gross Profit	40.2	37.3
Operating Expenses	37.4	34.6
Operating Profit	2.9	2.7
All Other Expenses	.5	—
Profit Before Taxes	2.4	2.7

Lady Lenore's cost of sales are a bit higher than normal but her total expenses are lower, resulting in a slightly higher than average profit before taxes.

Now that we've completed this surface analysis, let's really take Lady Lenore apart by using the RMA financial ratios. Notice that under each ratio there are three numbers. These represent quartile breaks. For example, in the "Current" row we see the numbers

$$3.4$$
$$2.3$$
$$1.5$$

One-fourth (25 percent, or the first quartile) of the businesses surveyed had a *current ratio* greater than 3.4; one-fourth were between 3.4 and 2.3. Thus 50 percent of the businesses were above 2.3 and 50 percent below it (25 percent between 2.3 and 1.5 and 25 percent below 1.5).

What's the current ratio? It's current assets divided by current liabilities and it measures how well or poorly a business can satisfy debts and payables on a short-term basis. Too low a ratio (below 1.5) means a business *in this industry* will have difficulty meeting its obligations. If the ratio is too high (above 3.4), the current assets are not being worked hard enough.

What's Lady Lenore's current ratio?

$$\frac{\text{current assets}}{\text{current liabilities}} = \frac{\$119,000}{\$\ 51,600} = 2.3$$

Is this good or bad? Well, it's neither. We need more information, more ratios to give us the complete story. The following table summarizes the 16 ratios with brief explanations. Look over this table first and then work through the example.

Lady Lenore's first two ratios, the current ratio and the quick ratio, are in line.

The sales-to-receivables ratio, however, is horrible. Lady Lenore needs to pay some real attention to collecting money from customers and not letting accounts remain uncollected. Of course, the other solution is to increase sales.

Cost-of-sales-to-inventory is a bit low but not out of the ballpark. If the ratio drops in the future, our business owner will have to start analyzing inventory to see if there are ways to increase turnover by managing slow-moving stock and instituting better buying practices.

Sales/working capital is low. Because current assets are within normal range and current liabilities are low, the ratio is low. Obviously if current liabilities increase, the value of working capital (current assets minus current liabilities) decreases, driving the ratio higher. Again, though, sales could also be increased.

Ratio 6, the so-called interest coverage, is within acceptable limits. As we

Ratio	How Calculated	Basic Meaning	RMA Median Value	Lady Lenore Value
1. Current	$\dfrac{\text{Current Assets}}{\text{Current Liabilities}}$	Measures the short-term liquidity of the business. Bankers get nervous when the ratio approaches 1.0	2.3	2.3
2. Quick	$\dfrac{\text{Current Assets-Inventory}}{\text{Current Liabilities}}$	A slightly more conservative measure of liquidity since inventory is taken out of current assets.	0.7	0.9
3. Sales/Receivables	$\dfrac{\text{Net Sales}}{\text{Accounts Receivable}}$	This is also called the receivables turnover because it measures the number of times receivables "turn over" in one year. The higher the number, the shorter the time between the sale and collection of cash.	27.1	8.9
4. Cost of Sales/Inventory	$\dfrac{\text{Cost of Sales}}{\text{Inventory}}$	Called inventory turnover, generally the higher it is the better; but too large a value could indicate shortages and poor buying practices.	3.2	2.6
5. Sales/Working Capital	$\dfrac{\text{Net Sales}}{\text{Current Assets-Current Liabilities}}$	A measurement of how efficiently short-term net capital is working in the business. Too low and capital is not being put to its best use; too high and company is operating too "thinly."	6.3	4.5
6. EBIT/Interest (EBIT = earnings before interest and taxes)	$\dfrac{\text{Profit Before Taxes + Interest}}{\text{Interest}}$	This is called "interest coverage," something that vitally interests a banker. Too low a value and the banker feels there are not enough earnings to protect the bank's "interest."	2.0	1.9
7. Cash Flow/Cur. Mat. LTD	$\dfrac{\text{Profit After Taxes + Depreciation}}{\text{Current Debt}}$	A measure of the ability of a company to service the current (one-year) portion of its long term debt.	2.1	1.1
8. Fixed/Worth	$\dfrac{\text{Net Fixed Assets}}{\text{Net Worth}}$	An efficiency ratio of how well investments plus accumulated profits (net worth) have gone to purchase buildings, equipment, furniture and fixtures.	0.3	0.6
9. Debt/Worth	$\dfrac{\text{Total Liabilities}}{\text{Net Worth}}$	The relationship between debt capital supplied by a lender and equity capital plus accumulated profits, the capital supplied by the owner(s). A low ratio generally means a business can borrow more.	1.2	2.7
10. % Profit/Net Worth	$\dfrac{\text{Profit Before Taxes}}{\text{Net Worth}} \times 100$	Demonstrates the return on the owner's investment.	12.5	19.0
11. % Profit/Total Assets	$\dfrac{\text{Profit Before Taxes}}{\text{Total Assets}} \times 100$	Return on the assets—how efficiently the assets are being used to make a profit.	5.3	5.1
12. Sales/Net Fixed Assets	$\dfrac{\text{Sales}}{\text{Net Fixed Assets}}$	A measure of the use of the physical assets. A low figure could mean heavily depreciated assets, even obsolete assets.	24.2	11.1
13. Sales/Total Assets	$\dfrac{\text{Sales}}{\text{Total Assets}}$	Same as above but involving all the assets.	2.6	1.9
14. % Depr./Sales	$\dfrac{\text{Annual Depreciation}}{\text{Sales}} \times 100$	Self-explanatory. This is an operating ratio to analyze current charges.	1.2	1.0
15. % Lease/ Sales	$\dfrac{\text{Rental Expenses}}{\text{Sales}} \times 100$	Same as above.	4.7	4.8
16. % Owner's Comp./Sales	$\dfrac{\text{Owner's Salary}}{\text{Sales}} \times 100$	Same as above.	5.0	6.5

saw in the balance sheet analysis, though, Lady Lenore has too much debt. Because higher debt produces higher interest charges, she would be unable to do additional borrowing. Ratio 7 is a tad low but, as we've said, debt is high, even the current portion of the long-term debt. Ratio 8, fixed/worth, is high primarily because her net worth is low.

The next ratio, debt/worth or the debt-to-equity ratio, again points to the fact that Lady Lenore has too much debt for its current structure and not enough equity.

Let's take ratios 10 and 11 together with another percentage we calculated earlier, profit before taxes, and look at them in summary form:

	RMA	Lady Lenore
% Profit/Sales	2.4	2.7
% Profit/Worth	12.5	19.0
% Profit/Assets	5.3	5.1

The business is profitable but an analyst could be misled by the profit/worth figure if it wasn't known that the company's net worth is below average.

Ratio 12, sales-to-net-fixed-assets, is interesting. If we look back at the balance sheet percentages, we see that the percentage of net fixed assets to total assets (17.5 percent) is only slightly higher than the average (15.7 percent). We have been hinting that sales may be a bit low and now we have some strong evidence, especially when we look at the next ratio, sales/total assets.

The so-called operating ratios, 14, 15, and 16, are in line.

What does all this analysis mean for the owner of Lady Lenore?

1. Immediate attention must be given to collecting accounts receivable. This means phone calls and letters. It also means that a business policy must be established regarding credit and collection.
2. She must examine her current policy regarding payables. Is she paying them too quickly?
3. A new marketing plan must be written to show how sales can be increased using existing assets and facilities. She can't borrow to do this. If sales can be increased and the fixed costs held relatively constant, then profit will increase and that, in turn, will increase net worth.

Ratio analysis is not a one-time affair. It goes on continually. You can't just run a few ratios and let it go at that; you need a significant number of them to tell a complete story.

Using Your Advisors

Keep your advisors, especially your banker, informed of what you are doing. Send regular financial reports and visit that person at least twice a year. Have regular reviews with your accountant, more frequently in the beginning. Learn to interpret and act on what the financial data is telling you. Hold annual reviews with your attorney and your insurance agent. Be prepared to call in a business consultant when you need help with marketing research or inventory control. If you use an advertising agency, meet with them to analyze the effectiveness of your business.

Final Advice

I said earlier that it isn't money that makes a business go. Money is only a lubricant to the overall machine. Of course, a machine won't run without proper lubrication, but it's not the be-all and end-all.

First, you must pay strict and constant attention to your market. I've watched longstanding businesses go belly-up because owners failed to notice that the needs of their customers were changing: the world changed but the business did not. Marketing research, like your business plan, isn't something you do once and forget. Both are continuous. If you can't meet customer demand at least as well as your competition, then you either limp along, never really getting out of the survival phase, or you fail. Neither is fun.

If you update your business plan every year, it forces you to re-examine your market, forecast your operations, and examine your finances in advance. The more you plan, the more you make the business just the way you want it. It isn't uncommon to find business owners who come within 5 percent of their financial projections after planning for two years or more. Be sure your banker and your investors receive copies of any new plans.

More business owners today discover that they gain a wider view of their ventures if they define the business both broadly and conceptually. Big companies began this move a number of years ago: a large producer of electric motors redefined their concept and decided they were in the automation business; the telephone company is telling us they're in the information business; a computer manufacturer wants you to know they're engaged in the knowledge business. Small businesses can and should do the same thing. A drug store is a health maintenance operation and hardware stores are becoming home improvement centers. The broader the concept, the more business opportunities occur for the entrepreneur.

Although you may have heard the term until you're tired of it, this is the information age. Successful entrepreneurs today know how to acquire information and how to use it. There have even been several books written strictly to help small business owners find information. The work by Gumpert and Timmons referenced earlier is one of the better examples. You need to become familiar with the sources of information of most help to you and your business, and you need to know how to use them.

Throughout this book I've stressed methodology as it applies to business. You establish your own methods as you gain experience. Some of these methods will work well; others won't and must be discarded. The point is not so much what initially works and what doesn't but that you're working toward an overall methodology that eventually allows the business to run smoothly and profitably.

James Howard, the founder of Country Business Services, stresses these concepts and makes an extremely convincing plea for quality in small business products and services. We have too much of the impermanent, the transient, and the obsolete. There's a need for quality and the willingness is there to pay for it on a larger scale than ever before.

We're becoming a decentralized society. People aren't ranging as far as they used to. There are more people living alone than ten years ago. The small computer is appearing in our homes; the term "electronic cottage" sprang into being several years ago. Put altogether, this decentralization means small businesses, more than ever before, will be localized. They'll also be more technological.

Probably the most important trend in small business, however, has nothing to do with plans or methods or analysis or technology. It has to do with the business owner. Borrowing a phrase from Emerson, "A business is the lengthening shadow of its owner." This means that the business itself reflects the values, taste, ethics, and integrity of the owner.

And that is the way it should be.

SBA Field Offices

Addresses and Commercial Telephone Numbers

Boston, Mass.   02110
  60 Batterymarch Street, 10th Floor
  (617) 223-3204

Boston, Mass.   02114
  150 Causeway St., 10th Floor
  (617) 223-3224

Holyoke, Mass.   01050
  302 High Street 4th Floor
  (413) 536-8770

Augusta, Maine   04330
  40 Western Avenue, Room 512
  (207) 622-6171

Concord, N.H.   03301
  55 Pleasant Street, Room 211
  (603) 224-4041

Hartford, Conn.   06103
  One Financial Plaza
  (203) 244-3600

Montpelier, Vt.   05602
  87 State Street, Room 204
  P.O. Box 605
  (802) 229-0538

Providence, R.I.   02903
  380 Westminster Mall
  (401) 351-7500

New York, N.Y.   10007
  26 Federal Plaza, Room 29-118
  (212) 264-7772

New York, N.Y.   10007
  26 Federal Plaza, Room 3100
  (212) 264-4355

Melville, N.Y.   11747
  401 Broad Hollow Road, Suite 322
  (516) 752-1626

Puerto Rico & Virgin Islands   00919
  Chardon and Bolivia Streets
  P.O. Box 1915
  (809) 753-4572

St. Thomas, V.I.   00801
  Veterans Drive, Room 283
  (809) 774-8530

Newark, N.J.   07102
  970 Broad St., Room 1635
  (201) 645-2434

Camden, N.J.   08104
  1800 East Davis Street
  (609) 757-5183

Syracuse, N.Y.   13260
  100 South Clinton Street, Room 1071
  (315) 423-5383

Buffalo, N.Y.   14202
  111 West Huron St., Room 1311
  (716) 846-4301

Elmira, N.Y.   14901
  180 State Street, Room 412
  (607) 733-4686

Albany, N.Y.   12210
  99 Washington Ave., Room 301
  Mezzanine
  (518) 472-6300

Rochester, N.Y.   14614
  100 State Street, Room 601
  (716) 263-6700

Philadelphia, Bala Cynwyd, Pa.   19004
  231 St. Asaphs Rd., Suite 646
  West Lobby
  (215) 596-5984

Philadelphia, Bala Cynwyd, Pa.   19004
  231 St. Asaphs Rd., Suite 400
  East Lobby
  (215) 596-5889

Harrisburg, Pa.   17101
  100 Chestnut Street, 3rd. Floor
  (717) 782-3840

Wilkes-Barre, Pa.   18702
  20 North Pennsylvania Avenue
  (717) 826-6497

Wilmington, Del.   19801
  844 King Street, Room 5207
  (302) 573-6294

Baltimore, Towson, Md.   21204
  8600 LaSalle Road, Room 630
  (301) 962-4392

Clarksburg, W.Va.   26301
  109 North 3rd St., Room 301
  (304) 623-5631

Charleston, W.Va.   25301
  Charleston National Plaza, Suite 628
  (304) 343-6181

Pittsburgh, Pa.   15222
  1000 Liberty Ave., Room 1401
  (412) 644-2780

Richmond, Va.   23240
  400 North 8th St., Room 3015
  P.O. Box 10126
  (804) 782-2617

Washington, D.C.   20417
  1030 15th St. N.W., Suite 250
  (202) 653-6963

Atlanta, Ga.   30309
  1375 Peachtree St., N.E., 5th Floor
  (404) 881-4943

Atlanta, Ga.   30309
  1720 Peachtree Street, N.W.
  6th Floor
  (404) 881-4325

Birmingham, Ala.   35205
  908 South 20th St., Room 202
  (205) 254-1344

Charlotte, N.C.   28202
  230 S. Tryon Street, Suite 700
  (704) 371-6111

Greenville, N.C.   27834
  215 South Evans Street, Room 206
  (919) 752-3798

Columbia, S.C.   29201
  1835 Assembly Street, 3rd Floor
  (803) 765-5376

Jackson, Miss.   39201
  100 West Capitol Street, Suite 322
  (601) 969-4371

Biloxi, Miss.   39530
  111 Fred Haise Blvd., 2nd Floor
  (601) 435-3676

Jacksonville, Fla.   32202
  400 West Bay St., Room 261
  P.O. Box 35067
  (904) 791-3782

Louisville, Ky.   40201
  600 Federal Pl., Room 188
  P.O. Box 3517
  (502) 582-5971

Miami, Coral Gables, Fla.   33134
  2222 Ponce De Leon Boulevard
  5th Floor
  (305) 350-5521

Tampa, Fla.   33602
  700 Twiggs Street, Suite 607
  (813) 228-2594

Nashville, Tenn.   37219
404 James Robertson Parkway
Suite 1012
(615) 251-5881

Knoxville, Tenn.   37902
502 South Gay St., Room 307
(615) 637-9300

Memphis, Tenn.   38103
167 North Main St., Room 211
(901) 521-3588

West Palm Beach, Fla.   33402
701 Clematis St., Room 229
(305) 659-7533

Chicago, Ill.   60604
219 South Dearborn St., Room 838
(312) 353-0355

Chicago, Ill.   60604
219 South Dearborn St., Room 437
(312) 353-4528

Springfield, Ill.   62701
One North, Old State Capital Plaza
(217) 525-4416

Cleveland, Ohio   44199
1240 East 9th St., Room 317
(216) 522-4180

Columbus, Ohio   43215
85 Marconi Boulevard
(614) 469-6860

Cincinnati, Ohio   45202
550 Main St., Room 5028
(513) 684-2814

Detroit, Mich.   48226
477 Michigan Ave.
(313) 226-6075

Marquette, Mich.   49855
540 W. Kaye Avenue
(906) 225-1108

Indianapolis, Ind.   46204
575 North Pennsylvania St.
Room 552
(317) 269-7272

Madison, Wisc.   53703
212 East Washington Ave., Room 213
(608) 264-5261

Milwaukee, Wisc.   53202
517 East Wisconsin Avenue, Room
246
(414) 291-3941

Eau Claire, Wisc.   54701
500 South Barstow St., Room B9AA
(715) 834-9012

Minneapolis, Minn.   55402
12 South 6th St.
(612) 725-2362

Dallas, Tex.   75235
1720 Regal Row, Room 230
(214) 767-7640

Dallas, Tex.   75242
1100 Commerce St., Room 3C36
(214) 767-0600

Marshall, Tex.   75670
100 South Washington Street
Room G-12
(214) 935-5255

Albuquerque, N.M.   87110
5000 Marble Avenue, N.E., Room 320
(505) 766-3433

Houston, Tex.   77002
500 Dallas Street
(713) 226-4343

Little Rock, Ark.   72201
320 West Capitol Ave., Savors
Fed. Bldg.
(501) 378-5876

Lubbock, Tex.   79401
1205 Texas Avenue, Room 712
(806) 762-7466

El Paso, Tex.   79902
4100 Rio Bravo, Suite 300
(915) 543-7580

Lower Rio Grande Valley
Harlingen, Tex.   78550
222 East Van Buren Street
P.O. Box 2567
(512) 423-4530

Corpus Christi, Tex.   78408
3105 Leopard Street, P.O. Box 9253
(512) 888-3333

New Orleans, La.   70113
1001 Howard Avenue, 17th Floor
(504) 589-6686

Shreveport, La.   71101
500 Fannin Street, Room 5B06
(318) 226-5196

Oklahoma City, Okla.   73102
200 N.W. 5th Street, Suite 670
(405) 231-4301

Tulsa, Okla.   74103
333 West Fourth Street, Room 3104
(918) 581-7495

San Antonio, Tex.   78206
727 East Durango Street
Room A-513
(512) 229-6250

Austin, Tex.   78701
300 East 8th Street
(512) 397-5288

Kansas City, Mo.   64106
911 Walnut St., 23rd Floor
(816) 374-5288

Kansas City, Mo.   64106
1150 Grande Ave., 5th Floor
(816) 374-3416

Des Moines, Iowa   50309
210 Walnut St., Room 749
(515) 284-4422

Omaha, Neb.   68102
19th & Farnum St., 2nd Floor
(402) 221-4691

St. Louis, Mo.   63101
One Mercantile Center, Suite 2500
(314) 425-4191

Wichita, Kans.   67202
110 East Waterman Street
(316) 267-6571

Denver, Colo.   80202
1405 Curtis Street, 22nd Floor
(303) 837-5763

Denver, Colo.   80202
721 19th Street
(303) 837-2607

Casper, Wyo.   82602
100 East B Street, Room 4001
P.O. Box 2839
(307) 265-5266

Fargo, N.D.   58108
657 2nd Ave., North, Room 218
P.O. Box 3086
(701) 237-5771

Helena, Mont.   59601
301 South Park Avenue, Room 528
Drawer 10054
(406) 449-5381

Salt Lake City, Utah   84138
125 South State St., Room 2237
(314) 425-5800

Sioux Falls, S.D.   57102
101 South Main Ave., Suite 101
(605) 336-2980

Rapid City, S.D.   57701
515 9th St., Room 246
(605) 343-5074

San Francisco, Calif.   94102
450 Golden Gate Ave.
P.O. Box 36044
(415) 556-7487

San Francisco, Calif.   94105
211 Main Street, 4th Floor
(415) 556-7490

Oakland, Calif.   94612
1515 Clay Street
(415) 273-7790

Fresno, Calif.   93712
1229 "N" St., P.O. Box 828
(209) 487-5189

Sacramento, Calif.   95825
2800 Cottage Way, Room 2535
(916) 484-4720

Las Vegas, Nev.   89101
301 E Stewart, P.O. Box 7525
Downtown Station
(702) 385-6611

Reno, Nev.   89505
50 South Virginia St., Room 308
P.O. Box 3216
(702) 784-5268

Honolulu, Hawaii 96850
   300 Ala Moana, Room 2213
   P.O. Box 50207
   (808) 546-8950

Agana, Guam 96910
   Pacific Daily News Bldg., Room 508,
   Martyr & O'Hara
   (671) 477-8420

Los Angeles, Calif. 90071
   350 S. Figueroa St., 6th Floor
   (213) 688-2956

Phoenix, Ariz. 85012
   3030 North Central Avenue
   Suite 1201
   (602) 241-2200

Tucson, Ariz. 85715
   301 West Congress Street, Room 3V
   (602) 762-6715

San Diego, Calif. 92188
   880 Front Street, Room 4-S-29
   (714) 293-5440

Seattle, Wash. 98104
   710 2nd Ave., 5th Floor
   (206) 442-5676

Seattle, Wash. 98174
   915 Second Ave., Room 1744
   (206) 442-5534

Anchorage, Alaska 99501
   1016 West 6th Ave., Suite 200
   (907) 271-4022

Fairbanks, Alaska 99701
   101 12th Avenue, Box 14
   Federal Bldg. & Courthouse
   (907) 452-1951

Boise, Idaho 83701
   1005 Main St., 2nd Floor
   (208) 334-2200

Portland, Oreg. 97204
   1220 S.W. Third Avenue, Room 676
   (503) 221-2682

Spokane, Wash. 99210
   West 920 Riverside Avenue
   Room, 651, P.O. Box 2167
   (509) 456-5310

U.S. Department of Commerce District Offices

ALABAMA

* **Birmingham**—Gayle C. Shelton, Jr., Director, Suite 200-201, 908 South 20th Street, 35205, Area Code 205 Tel 254-1331, FTS 229-1331

ALASKA

Anchorage—Edgar J. Rojas, Director, 701 C Street, P.O. Box 32, 99513, Area Code 907 Tel 271-5041, FTS 8 907 271-5041

ARIZONA

Phoenix—Donald W. Fry, Director, Suite 2750 Valley Bank Center, 201 North Central Avenue 85073, Area Code 602 Tel 261-3285, FTS 261-3285

ARKANSAS

Little Rock—Lon J. Hardin, Director, Suite 635, Savers Federal Building, 320 W. Capitol Avenue, 72201, Area Code 501 Tel 378-5794, FTS 740-5794

CALIFORNIA

Los Angeles—Daniel J. Young, Director, Room 800, 11777 San Vicente Boulevard 90049, Area Code 213 Tel 209-6707, FTS 793-6707

· **San Diego**—110 West C Street, 92101, Area Code 714 Tel 293-5395

* **San Francisco**—Betty D. Neuhart, Director, Federal Building, Box 36013, 450 Golden Gate Avenue 94102. Area Code 415 Tel 556-5860, FTS 556-5868

COLORADO

* **Denver**—Donald L. Schilke, Director, Room 119, U.S. Customhouse, 721-19th Street, 80202, Area Code 303 Tel 837-3246, FTS 327-3246

CONNECTICUT

* **Hartford**—Eric B. Outwater, Director, Room 610-B, Federal Office Building, 450 Main Street 06103, Area Code 203 Tel 244-3530, FTS 244-3530

DELAWARE

Serviced by Philadelphia District Office

DISTRICT OF COLUMBIA

Serviced by Baltimore District Office

FLORIDA

Miami—Ivan A. Cosimi, Director, Suite 224, Federal Building, 51 S.W. First Avenue 33130, Area Code 305 Tel 350-5267, FTS 350-5267

· **Clearwater**—128 North Osceola Avenue 33515, Area Code 813 Tel 461-0011

· **Jacksonville**—3 Independent Drive, 32202, Area Code 904 Tel 791-2796, FTS 946-2796

· **Tallahassee**—Collins Bldg., Rm. G-20 32304, Area Code 904 Tel 488-6469, FTS 946-4320

GEORGIA

Atlanta—Daniel M. Paul, Director, Suite 600, 1365 Peachtree Street, N.E. 30309, Area Code 404 Tel 881-7000, FTS 257-7000

Savannah—James W. McIntire, Director, 27 E Bay Street P.O. Box 9746, 31401, Area Code 912 Tel 944-4204, FTS 248-4204

HAWAII

Honolulu—Steven K. Craven, Director, 4106 Federal Building, P.O. Box 50026, 300 Ala Moana Boulevard 96850, Area Code 808 Tel 546-8694, FTS 8 808-546-8694

IDAHO

Serviced by Salt Lake City District Office

ILLINOIS

Chicago—Joseph F. Christiano, Director, 1406 Mid Continental Plaza Building, 55 East Monroe Street 60603, Area Code 312 Tel 353-4450, FTS 353-4450

· **Commerce Business Daily**
Room 1304, 433 West Van Buren Street 60607, Area Code 312 Tel 353-2950

INDIANA

Indianapolis—Mel R. Sherar, Director, 357 U.S. Courthouse & Federal Office Building, 46 East Ohio Street 46204, Area Code 317 Tel 269-6214, FTS 331-6214

IOWA

Des Moines—Jesse N. Durden, Director, 817 Federal Building, 210 Walnut Street 50309, Area Code 515 Tel 284-4222, FTS 862-4222

KANSAS

Wichita (Kansas City, Missouri District)—P.O. Box 48, Wichita State University, 67208, Area Code 316 Tel 269-6160, FTS 752-6160

KENTUCKY

Louisville—Donald R. Henderson, Director, Room 636B, U.S. Post Office and Courthouse Building 40202, Area Code 502 Tel 582-5066, FTS 352-5066

LOUISIANA

New Orleans—Raymond E. Eveland, Director, 432 International Trade Mart, No. 2 Canal Street 70130, Area Code 504 Tel 589-6546, FTS 682-6546

MAINE

· **Augusta (Boston, Massachusetts District)**—1 Memorial Circle, Casco Bank Bldg. 04330, Area Code 207 Tel 622-8249, FTS 833-6249

MARYLAND

Baltimore—Carroll F. Hopkins, Director, 415 U.S. Customhouse, Gay and Lombard Streets 21202, Area Code 301 Tel 962-3560, FTS 922-3560

MASSACHUSETTS

Boston—Francis J. O'Connor, Director, 10th Floor, 441 Stuart Street 02116, Area Code 617 Tel 223-2312, FTS 223-2312

MICHIGAN

Detroit—Raymond R. Riesgo, Director, 445 Federal Building, 231 West Lafayette 48226, Area Code 313 Tel 226-3650, FTS 226-3650

· **Grand Rapids**—300 Monroe N.W., Rm. 409 49503, Area Code 616 Tel 456-2411, FTS 372-2411

MINNESOTA

Minneapolis—Director, (Vacant) 218 Federal Building, 110 South Fourth Street 55401, Area Code 612 Tel 725-2133, FTS 725-2133

· DENOTES TRADE SPECIALIST AT POST OR DUTY STATION
* DENOTES REGIONAL OFFICE WITH SUPERVISORY REGIONAL RESPONSIBILITIES

MISSISSIPPI

Jackson—Mark E. Spinney, Director, Jackson Mall Office Ctr., Ste. 3230, 300 Woodrow Wilson Blvd., 39213, Area Code 601 Tel 960-4388, FTS 490-4388

MISSOURI

* **St. Louis**—Donald R. Loso, Director, 120 South Central Avenue 63105, Area Code 314 Tel 425-3302-4, FTS 279-3302

Kansas City—James D. Cook, Director, Room 1840, 601 East 12th Street 64106, Area Code 816 Tel 374-3142, FTS 758-3142

MONTANA

Serviced by Denver District Office

NEBRASKA

Omaha—George H. Payne, Director, Empire State Bldg., 1st Floor, 300 South 19th Street, 68102, Area Code 402 Tel 221-3664, FTS 864-3664

NEVADA

Reno—Joseph J. Jeremy, Director, 1755 E. Plumb Lane, #152, 89502, Area Code 702 Tel 784-5203, FTS 470-5203

NEW HAMPSHIRE

Serviced by Boston District Office

NEW JERSEY

* **Trenton**—Thomas J. Murray, Director, Capitol Plaza, 8th Fl., 240 West State St., 08608, Area Code 609 Tel 989-2100, FTS 483-2100

NEW MEXICO

Albuquerque—William E. Dwyer, Director, 505 Marquette Ave., NW, Suite 1015, 87102, Area Code 505 Tel 766-2386, FTS 474-2386

NEW YORK

Buffalo—Robert F. Magee, Director, 1312 Federal Building, 111 West Huron Street 14202, Area Code 716 Tel 846-4191, FTS 437-4191

New York—Arthur C. Rutzen, Director, Room 3718, Federal Office Building, 26 Federal Plaza, Foley Square 10278, Area Code 212 Tel 264-0634, FTS 264-0600

NORTH CAROLINA

* **Greensboro**—Joel B. New, Director, 203 Federal Building, West Market Street, P.O. Box 1950 27402, Area Code 919 Tel 378-5345, FTS 699-5345

NORTH DAKOTA

Serviced by Omaha District Office

OHIO

* **Cincinnati**—Gordon B. Thomas, Director, 9504 Federal Office Building, 550 Main Street 45202, Area Code 513 Tel 684-2944, FTS 684-2944

Cleveland—Zelda W. Milner, Director, Room 600, 666 Euclid Avenue 44114, Area Code 216 Tel 522-4750. FTS 942-4750

OKLAHOMA

Oklahoma City—Ronald L. Wilson, Director, 4024 Lincoln Boulevard 73105, Area Code 405 Tel 231-5302, FTS 736-5302

· **Tulsa**—440 S. Houston Street 74127, Area Code 918 Tel 581-7650, FTS 736-7650

OREGON

Portland—Lloyd R. Porter, Director, Room 618, 1220 S.W. 3rd Avenue 97204, Area Code 503 Tel 221-3001, FTS 423-3001

PENNSYLVANIA

Philadelphia—Robert E. Kistler, Director, 9448 Federal Building, 600 Arch Street 19106 Area Code 215 Tel 597-2866, FTS 597-2866

Pittsburgh—William M. Bradley, Director, 2002 Federal Building, 1000 Liberty Avenue 15222, Area Code 412 Tel 644-2850, FTS 722-2850

PUERTO RICO

San Juan (Hato Rey)—J. Enrique Vilella, Director, Room 659-Federal Building 00918, Area Code 809 Tel 753-4555, Ext. 555, FTS 8-809-753-4555

RHODE ISLAND

· **Providence (Boston, Massachusetts District)**—7 Jackson Walkway 02903, Area Code 401 Tel 277-2605, ext. 22, FTS 838-4482

SOUTH CAROLINA

Columbia—Johnny E. Brown, Director, Strom Thurmond Fed. Bldg., Suite 172, 1835 Assembly Street 29201, Area Code 803 Tel 765-5345, FTS 677-5345

· **Charleston**—505 Federal Building, 334 Meeting Street 29403, Area Code 803 Tel 677-4361, FTS 677-4361

· **Greenville**—P.O. Box 5823, Station B, 29606, Area Code 803 Tel 235-5919

SOUTH DAKOTA

Serviced by Omaha District Office

TENNESSEE

Nashville—James Charlet, Director, Suite 1427, One Commerce Place, 37239, Area Code 615 Tel 251-5161, FTS 852-5161

· **Memphis**—3693 Central Ave., 38111, Area Code 901 Tel 521-4826, FTS 222-4826

TEXAS

* **Dallas**—C. Carmon Stiles, Director, Room 7A5, 1100 Commerce Street 75242, Area Code 214 Tel 767-0542, FTS 729-0542

Houston—Felicito C. Guerrero, Director, 2625 Federal Bldg., Courthouse, 515 Rusk Street 77002, Area Code 713 Tel 229-2578, FTS 526-4578

UTAH

Salt Lake City—Stephen P. Smoot, Director, U.S. Courthouse, 350 S. Main Street 84101, Area Code 801 Tel 524-5116, FTS 588-5116

VERMONT

Serviced by Boston District Office

VIRGINIA

Richmond—Philip A. Ouzts, Director, 8010 Federal Bldg., 400 North 8th Street, 23240, Area Code 804 Tel 771-2246, FTS 925-2246

· **(Fairfax County) Dunn Loring**—8100 Oak St. Ste. 32, 22027, Area Code 703 Tel 573-9460, FTS 235-1519

WASHINGTON

Seattle—Eric C. Silberstein, Director, Room 706, Lake Union Building, 1700 Westlake Avenue North 98109, Area Code 206 Tel 442-5616, FTS 399-5615

WEST VIRGINIA

Charleston—Roger L. Fortner, Director, 3000 New Federal Building, 500 Quarrier Street 25301, Area Code 304 Tel 347-5123, ext. 375, FTS 930-5123, 5124, 5125

WISCONSIN

Milwaukee—(Vacant), Federal Bldg., U.S. Courthouse, 517 East Wisconsin Avenue 53202, Area Code 414 Tel 291-3473, FTS 362-3473

WYOMING

Cheyenne—(Vacant) 8007 O'Mahoney Federal Center, 2120 Capitol Avenue 82001, Area Code 307 Tel 772-2151, FTS 328-2151

· **DENOTES TRADE SPECIALIST AT POST OR DUTY STATION**
* **DENOTES REGIONAL OFFICE WITH SUPERVISORY REGIONAL RESPONSIBILITIES**

Business Plan
Appropriate Tools, Inc.

APPENDIX C

Prepared by: H. A. Finnell
Date: January 31, 1983

SUMMARY

Appropriate Tools, Inc. (ATI) is a new manufacturing company to be located in Marshfield, Wisconsin. The firm will initially produce and market a "Gardener's Starter Kit" consisting of a trowel, hand cultivator, spade, garden rake, and basic gardening book. The kit is designed for those new to basic gardening as well as those desiring quality tools. ATI's primary market is new homeowners, especially those in suburban areas. The kit will be marketed through hardware and garden supply wholesalers (distributors) who then sell directly to retail outlets. While single tools abound in these stores, there are currently no complete kits of quality hand gardening tools available.

ATI will also develop other long-lasting hand tools for the novice and expert gardener. The company will conduct research into the use of each tool and introduce only those models exhibiting significant advantages in service and durability. ATI is aiming for the top end of the market. ATI's founder, Harold A. Finnell, has an extensive background in hand tool marketing; he is assisted by James C. Hardy, who has substantial engineering and production experience.

PURPOSE

The purpose of this prospectus is to raise $45,000 in equity funds (30,000 shares at $1.50 per share) from private investors and to secure debt financing of $150,000 at commercial lending rates. Minimum equity investment is $3,000.

TABLE OF CONTENTS

I. THE BUSINESS
  A. Business Description
  B. Products
    1. Description of Product Line
    2. Proprietary Considerations
  C. Management Plan
    1. Organizational Form and Structure
    2. Resumés of Key People
    3. Staffing Plan
    4. Supporting Services
  D. Operations Plan
    1. Facilities and Equipment
    2. Plans for Growth and Expansion
    3. Overall Schedule
    4. Process Description
  E. Risks

II. MARKETING PLAN
  A. Marketing Research
    1. Description of the Market
    2. Industry Trends
    3. Target Market
    4. Competition
  B. Objectives and Strategy
  C. Pricing Policy
  D. Sales Terms
  E. Method of Sales and Distribution
  F. Customer Service
  G. Advertising and Promotion
  H. Forecasts

III. FINANCIAL DATA
  A. Proposal
  B. Use of Proceeds
  C. Opening Day Balance Sheet
  D. Cash Flow Projections
  E. Pro Forma Income Statements
  F. Breakeven Analysis

I. THE BUSINESS

A. Business Description

1. Name. The name of the business is Appropriate Tools, Incorporated.
2. Location. The proposed location is 420 Elm Street, Marshfield, Wisconsin.
3. Physical Facilities. ATI plans to lease a one-story, industrially zoned building consisting of 3,500 square feet of manufacturing space and 1,400 square feet of office space and storage facilities. The building has ample electrical service and a 20-hp air compressor.

B. Products

1. Description of Product Line. ATI's initial product offering is the "Gardener's Starter Kit," which includes a trowel, cultivator, spade, garden rake, and basic gardening book explaining the proper use of these new-design, high quality tools. All implements have replaceable wooden handles fitted to steel working ends; the tools and the gardening book are included in an attractive sturdy plastic box suitable for storage. The retail price for the kit is $49.95.
2. Proprietary Considerations. Although none of the tool designs are patentable, and they therefore could be copied, ATI will have a reasonable lead time on competition. Also, no other manufacturer or distributor uses a kit approach which includes a gardening book. Thus, ATI not only furnishes improved tools, but also information.

C. Management Plan

1. Organizational Form and Structure. Appropriate Tools, Inc., is a Wisconsin corporation chartered on June 18, 1982, with Harold A. Finnell as president and treasurer and James C. Hardy as vice president. Mr. Finnell is primarily responsible for marketing and finance whereas Mr. Hardy is in charge of quality control, purchasing, engineering, and manufacturing. Stock ownership is as follows:

H. A. Finnell	40,000 shares
J. C. Hardy	10,000 shares

Mr. Finnell has a 12-month option on 5,000 additional shares at $1.00 each. ATI will begin operation with one administrative and four production people in addition to Messrs. Finnell and Hardy.

2. Resumés of Key People

Harold A. Finnell earned a B.S. degree in marketing from Ohio State University and an M.B.A. from the University of Indiana. From 1971 to 1974 he was employed by "Horticulture" magazine where he became the advertising manager. From 1973 to 1974 he increased advertising revenues 28 percent by conducting an aggressive campaign to secure new advertisers for the publication. In 1975, Mr. Finnell joined True Temper Tools (Ferndale, Wisconsin) as national sales manager. His responsibilities included relationships with both distributors and retail outlets. As vice president of marketing for True Temper from 1978 to 1982, he secured over 1,000 new retail outlets resulting in a 156% increase in sales during that period. Mr. Finnell resigned his position in 1982 to form ATI.

James C. Hardy holds a bachelor's degree in mechanical engineering from Purdue University. Mr. Hardy has over six years' manufacturing and assembly experience as a production manager for Allegheny Castings (Pittsburgh, Pennsylvania) and as the manager of production planning for True Temper Tools. He will join ATI on a full-time basis when the funding is in place.

3. Staffing Plan. ATI will begin operation with seven people. The addition of further administrative and production personnel will take place according to the following schedule:

Period Ending	Total Personnel Administrative	Production
First six months	1	4
First year	1	6
First eighteen months	2	12
Second year	3	18

4. Supporting Services.

Attorney:	John Squiers, Esq., 425 W. Main Street, Marshfield, Wisconsin. (also clerk of the corporation)
Accountant:	Jane Parsons, CPA, 482 W. Main Street, Marshfield, Wisconsin.
Insurance:	Parker and Cerano, 24 South Street, Marshfield, Wisconsin.
Advertising:	Admete, Inc., 1420 Pepper Avenue, Milwaukee, Wisconsin.

D. Operations Plan

1. Facilities and Equipment. The next page shows the initial floor plan for ATI. In addition to desks, chairs, work tables and filing cabinets, the following equipment is needed for production and shipping:

> Hand tools
> Air grinders (portable)
> Arbor press
> Shrink wrap machine
> Banding machine
> Air stenciling device

2. Plans For Growth and Expansion. The proposed building will serve ATI's needs for three to five years. Because early production levels of the Starter Kit utilize less than 50 percent of the available space, as demand increases, additional assembly space can be created within the existing plant. A paint booth (shown in the floor plan) will be added to the operation approximately 15 months after manufacturing begins.

3. Overall Schedule. During the first year of operation, the major manufacturing objective is to insure: 1) that a smooth growth in production occurs; 2) that ATI learns which assembly methods work best; 3) that quality is maintained; and 4) that unit costs are reduced as a function of increased volume. During the second year, new tools will be added to the manufacturing process—hoes, pitchforks, and hand pruners. In the third year, ATI will begin production of wheel cultivators and edgers.

4. Process Description. ATI's manufacturing process is primarily one of assembly. The metal parts for the tools are made to ATI's specifications by outside stamping and forging suppliers. Similarly, wooden handles are purchased from wood-working vendors. All incoming parts are inspected and either accepted or rejected. Acceptable parts are placed in storage until needed. Once assembled, the tools are stenciled with ATI's logo and moved to the packaging area where four tools are placed in a sturdy storage box; the entire kit is then shrink-wrapped for shipment. The standard shipment is 50 kits banded to a 4' × 4' pallet. Pallet shipment is made by motor carrier; shipments of separate kits (non-palletized) are by UPS.

E. Risks

There are no abnormal risks inherent in ATI. A large market exists for gardening equipment; the production of ATI tools is simple; there are many suppliers to furnish quality metal and wooden parts. The major risk lies with the willingness of an amateur, suburban gardener to spend fifty dollars for four rather simple tools in a kit,

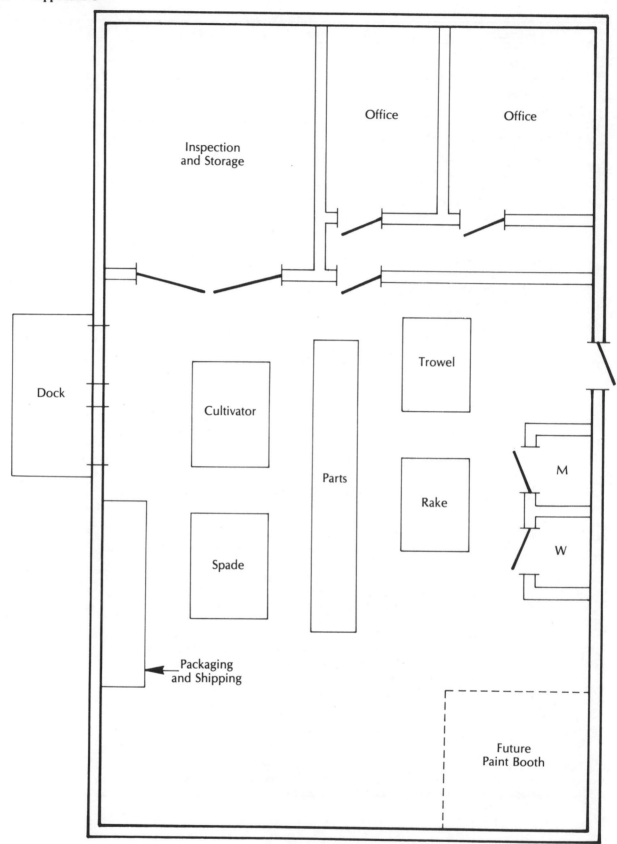

APPROPRIATE TOOLS, INC.
Floor Plan

especially when the kit is displayed in hardware and garden supply stores alongside separate, less expensive tools. The idea of quality, utility, and long life must appeal to the customer and there must be enough customers to support ATI's planned growth.

Because ATI has not proven itself in the marketplace, investors must realize they may stand a high probability of losing all or a major portion of their investment.

A. **Marketing Research**

1. Description of the Market. Over $250,000,000 annually is spent on hand gardening implements. Although there is a move towards mechanized equipment (roto-tillers, mulchers, weed cutters), the small-time horticulturist and gardener still favors working in the soil with his or her hands. ATI demographics indicate there are over two million serious part-time gardeners, and these individuals tend to be in the upper ($50,000) family income levels. Although many of these people may begin gardening with tools costing a few dollars, they are often disappointed with the service that these tools deliver and seek out higher quality implements.

2. Industry Trends. Shipments of all lawn and garden equipment (SIC 3524), including power equipment, have their ups and downs, with the industry showing a decline through the late 1970's and early 1980's. This decline follows housing starts in the United States summarized below:

Year	Housing Starts (units)
1977	1,987,100
1978	2,020,300
1979	1,745,100
1980	1,292,200
1981	1,084,200
1982	636,000

The National Association of Home Builders estimates there will be 833,000 housing starts in 1983, an upturn in the market after a steady, four-year decline. One major factor in the long decline was high home mortgage rates which have now abated.

Another factor which boosts sales of hand tools over sales of powered equipment is the trend toward smaller lot size. As a result of inflationary home building prices and higher land prices, more intensive land use has become a common practice to keep new home prices within reach of more of the market. According to the Bureau of the Census, the median lot size from 1976 to 1981 has decreased steadily:

Year	Median Lot Size (square feet)
1976	10,125
1977	9,870
1978	9,790
1979	9,580
1980	9,180
1981	8,650

Home size over the same period has remained relatively constant.

According to the U.S. Department of Commerce's *U.S. Industrial Outlook 1983:*

"Housing starts are projected to increase 14 percent annually between 1982 and 1987. . . . In the same period, disposable personal income after inflation is expected to grow 2.3 percent annually.

"Given these rates of change, historical patterns suggest that shipments of lawn and garden equipment will increase 6.6 percent annually between 1982 and 1987, after adjustment for inflation. Part of the reason for this dramatic rate of growth will be that shipments were so depressed in 1981 and 1982. Thus, the industry is starting with a smaller base. Ship-

II. MARKETING PLAN

ments in 1987 are estimated to be 37 percent larger than in 1982, after adjustment for inflation, but they will still be below the 1979 level."

ATI further believes the sale of hand garden tools will outstrip the rate of growth for the lawn and garden equipment industry as a whole.

3. Target Market. ATI's target market is the suburban gardener in the upper income bracket. We do not feel the Starter Kit will sell primarily to first-time tool buyers because those buyers tend to purchase less expensive single tools. However, when these buyers discover that inexpensive tools do not hold up, they replace them with high quality, long-lasting implements.

Although specific data on ATI's target market are unavailable, we feel there are 2,000,000 Americans in this category.

4. Competition. The list of companies offering hand garden tools is too numerous to catalog. There are domestic companies (True Temper, Stanley) and many foreign imports, primarily from Korea and Taiwan. Prices vary widely. For example, hand trowels and cultivators are priced from $1.19 to over $3.00; spades and rakes from under $10.00 to over $30.00 There are also firms who sell tools by mail order—Garden Way, Smith & Hawken, Green Mountain Tools. None of these companies, however, offer the kit form ATI will introduce.

B. Objectives and Strategy

During the first two years of operation, ATI will concentrate on establishing relations with garden supply and hardware distributors. There are over 10,000 of these distributors nationwide who supply goods to hardware stores, home centers, and garden supply stores. The goal is to have 300 distributors for the Starter Kit by the end of the first year and 750 by the end of the second. Mass mailings will be made to distributors, and advertisements placed in gardening magazines. ATI will furnish interested distributors with one Starter Kit for their initial analysis. ATI believes its 20 percent margin for distributors and 30 percent margin for dealers (stores), coupled with a lifetime product guarantee, is attractive.

During the third year and with the addition of more tools to ATI's line, the company will begin a mail order business and conduct negotiations with mass merchandisers such as Ward, Sears, and J.C. Penney. There will be 1,000 distributors by the end of the third year.

C. Pricing Policy

The pricing for the Starter Kit is as follows:

Suggested retail price	$49.95
Price to dealer (store)	$34.95
Price to distributor	$27.95

Although the retail price for the kit may seem high—a consumer can purchase a separate trowel, cultivator, spade, and rake for under $30.00—the marketing research carried out by ATI with consumer panels demonstrates that those in higher income levels will pay for quality. The price to distributors of $27.95 is for the purchase of 10 kits or less at any one time. ATI will negotiate lower prices for large quantity purchases.

D. Sales Terms

Terms to distributors will be net 30 days.

E. Method of Sales and Distribution

Sales for the first two years will be strictly to distributors who then re-sell to stores. ATI is willing to discuss exclusive arrangements (protected territories) with distributors in return for minimum guaranteed sales levels.

F. Customer Service

ATI offers the consumer a lifetime guarantee for its tools. If an ATI tool breaks or otherwise does not perform its stated function, ATI will replace it. The customer simply mails the defective tool to ATI along with proof of purchase. This guarantee is unconditional.

G. Advertising and Promotion

Admete, Inc., of Milwaukee, will manage advertising for ATI. During the first nine months of operation, promotional literature will be mailed to prospective distributors. To help distributors in their contacts with the retail establishments, point-of-sale brochures will be made available. After the first nine months, monthly advertisements will appear in "Hardware Age" and "Garden Dealer" to further acquaint retailers with the concept of the Starter Kit. Any retailer writing directly to ATI will be given the name and address of the nearest distributor.

After eighteen months, the advertising will focus directly on the consumer. Ads will be placed in "Horticulture" and "Organic Gardening" magazines; their main purpose will be to create an awareness of the ATI Starter Kit so gardeners will ask for it by name at their local hardware store, home center, or garden shop. The lifetime guarantee and quality of the tools will be stressed.

In the third year of operation, ads will promote ATI's tool catalog to help establish the mail order portion of the business.

H. Forecasts

| | Starter Kits | | Other Tools | Mail Order | Total |
	Units	Dollars	Other Tools	Mail Order	Sales
Year 1	15,000	$419,250	—	—	$ 419,250
Year 2	25,000	698,750	$100,000	—	798,750
Year 3	30,000	838,500	220,000	$50,000	1,108,500

III. FINANCIAL DATA

A. Proposal

See "Purpose" section at the beginning of the business plan.

B. Use of Proceeds

Sources of Funds

Equity investment of H. A. Finnell	$ 40,000
Equity investment of J. C. Hardy	10,000
Other equity	45,000
Bank Loan	150,000
	$245,000

Use of Proceeds

Purchase of assets	$ 31,800
Beginning inventory	25,000
Working capital	188,200
	$245,000

C. Opening Day Balance Sheet

ASSETS		LIABILITIES	
Cash	$ 88,900	Accounts Payable	$ 18,700
Inventory	25,000	Long-Term Debt	75,000
Fixed Assets	31,800	Stockholder's Equity	65,000
Other Assets	13,000		$158,700
	$158,700		

D. Cash Flow Projections

NOTES TO THE CASH FLOW PROJECTIONS:

1. Months have been designated by number (1, 2, 3 . . .) rather than by name (Feb., Mar., Apr. . . .) because ATI will begin operation as soon as funding is obtained.
2. Expense category number 14, outside services, consists primarily of advertising agency fees. Expenses for printing and mailing are shown in category number 17, advertising.
3. Bank loan repayment is based on $150,000 borrowed at 14 percent for 15 years. Monthly payment is $1,997.61 (rounded to $2,000). The bank loan will be drawn down in the first two months, $75,000 each month.

MONTHLY CASH FLOW PROJECTION

Name of Business: **Appropriate Tools, Inc.**   Address: **420 Elm Street**

		Year: 1983-1984	1	2	3	4	5
		Month	1	2	3	4	5
1		Your investment	50000				
2	Less:	Startup costs	81100				
3							
4		Beginning cash	(31100)	36300	102500	96800	71500
5	Plus:	Cash sales	—	—	—	500	1000
6		Collection of A/R	4000	11000	13500	17000	20000
7		Loans, other (specify)	75000	75000	—	—	—
8			15000	15000	15000	—	—
9	Total available cash		62900	137300	131000	114300	92500
10	Expenses						
11		Purchase of inventory	—	11500	13700	24100	18400
12		Employee wages	5200	5200	5200	5200	5200
13		Payroll taxes & exp.	1900	1900	1900	1900	1900
14		Outside services	2000	1800	1000	500	500
15		Business suplies	900	400	300	300	200
16		Repairs and maint.	—	100	100	—	—
17		Advertising	4000	3200	2100	1500	1000
18		Car, delivery, travel	400	300	300	300	500
19		Acctg. & legal	1500	600	300	200	200
20		Rent	1500	1500	1500	1500	1500
21		Telephone	800	700	600	600	600
22		Utilities	300	300	300	300	300
23		Insurance	1200	200	100	—	—
24		Taxes	—	—	—	—	—
25		Equipment	—	—	—	—	10000
26		Other : Factory Supplies	400	600	500	400	300
27							
28		Loan repayment	2000	2000	2000	2000	2000
29		Miscellaneous	1000	1000	800	500	400
30		Owner's withdrawal	3500	3500	3500	3500	3500
31	Total expenses		26600	34800	34200	42800	46500
32	Ending cash (9 less 31)		36300	102500	96800	71500	46000
33							
34							
35							

Marshfield WI   Prepared by: H.A. Finnell   Date: 1/31/83

6	7	8	9	10	11	12	Total 12 Months	
							50000	1
							81100	2
								3
46000	29000	6200	11400	8300	600	15200		4
1000	1000	1000	1000	1000	1500	2000	10000	5
23500	27000	31000	38000	46000	48000	62500	341500	6
—	—	—	—	—	—	—	150000	7
—	—	—	—	5000	—	—	45000	8
70500	57000	38200	50400	60300	50100	79700	546500	9
								10
21600	29500	4000	18600	21400	12100	8000	182900	11
5200	7300	7300	7300	7300	7300	7300	75000	12
1900	2400	2400	2400	2400	2400	2400	25800	13
600	200	1500	300	400	400	400	9600	14
200	300	400	500	500	500	500	5000	15
200	200	—	—	300	300	200	1400	16
1000	1000	1200	1300	2000	1400	1800	21500	17
500	600	600	500	500	600	600	5700	18
200	200	200	200	1200	500	300	5600	19
1500	1500	1500	1500	1500	1500	1500	18000	20
500	500	500	500	500	500	500	6800	21
300	300	300	300	300	300	300	3600	22
600	—	—	1800	1800	—	—	5700	23
1000	—	—	—	—	—	3000	4000	24
—	—	—	—	12500	—	—	22500	25
300	200	500	500	600	600	600	5500	26
								27
2000	2000	2000	2000	2000	2000	2000	24000	28
400	600	400	400	500	500	800	7300	29
3500	4000	4000	4000	4000	4000	4000	45000	30
41500	50800	26800	42100	59700	34900	34200	474900	31
29000	6200	11400	8300	600	15200	45500	71600	32
								33
								34
								35

CASH FLOW PROJECTIONS (Second and Third Years)

Name of Business: Appropriate Tools Inc.   Address:

			Year: 2				
			Qtr. 1	Qtr. 2	Qtr. 3	Qtr. 4	Year Totals
1							
2							
3							
4		Beginning cash	45500	13100	23500	39300	
5	Plus:	Cash sales	10000	15000	15000	20000	60000
6		Collection of A/R	156000	153000	166000	214000	689000
7		Loans, other (specify)	—	—	—	—	—
8			—	—	—	—	—
9	Total available cash		211500	181100	204500	273300	870400
10	Expenses						
11		Purchase of inventory	71000	60500	68000	101000	300500
12		Employee wages	43800	38700	42100	62000	186600
13		Payroll taxes & exp.	12100	11100	11800	16000	51000
14		Outside services	7000	5000	3000	6800	21800
15		Business suplies	1500	1500	1000	1600	5600
16		Repairs and maint.	1000	1500	500	1800	4800
17		Advertising	6000	5000	4000	7500	22500
18		Car, delivery, travel	2000	2000	1500	2000	7500
19		Acctg. & legal	2400	1000	1000	2800	7200
20		Rent	4500	4500	4500	4500	18000
21		Telephone	1500	1500	1500	1500	6000
22		Utilities	1200	1200	1200	1200	4800
23		Insurance	1400	600	800	2300	5100
24		Taxes	—	500	500	1800	2800
25		Equipment	18000	—	—	—	18000
26		Other	2000	1000	1800	1500	6300
27							
28		Loan repayment	6000	6000	6000	6000	24000
29		Miscellaneous	3000	2000	2000	2000	9000
30		Owner's withdrawal	14000	14000	14000	14000	56000
31	Total expenses		198400	157600	165200	236300	757500
32	Ending cash (9 less 31)		13100	23500	39300	37000	112900
33							
34							
35							

Prepared by: Date:

	Qtr. 1	Qtr. 2	Qtr. 3	Qtr. 4	Year Totals		
			Year: 3				
4	37000	22300	4600	27700			
5	20000	25000	35000	40000	120000		
6	208000	220000	260000	287000	975000		
7	—	—	—	—	—		
8	—	—	—	—	—		
9	265000	267300	295000	354700	1095000		
10							
11	93700	118000	120000	137000	468700		
12	65000	65000	70000	87500	287500		
13	17000	17000	18500	22200	74700		
14	7000	6000	6000	6000	25000		
15	1800	2000	2000	2000	7800		
16	1000	1000	1000	1000	4000		
17	7500	7500	7500	7500	30000		
18	1800	2000	2000	2000	7800		
19	2100	1800	1500	2300	7700		
20	4500	4500	4500	4500	18000		
21	1800	1800	1800	1800	7200		
22	1400	1400	1400	1400	5600		
23	2100	1400	1800	2000	7300		
24	1000	2000	1000	2000	6000		
25	8700	5000	—	10000	23700		
26	1800	1800	1800	1800	7200		
27							
28	6000	6000	6000	6000	24000		
29	2500	2500	2500	2500	10000		
30	16000	16000	18000	18000	68000		
31	242700	262700	267300	317500	1090200		
32	22300	4600	27700	37200	4800		

4. Mr. Finnell exercises his 5,000 share option in month 10.
5. Outside equity investment of $45,000 is shown as occurring over the first three months in equal installments.

Startup Costs

1. Real estate, furniture, fixtures, machinery, equipment:
   a. Purchase price (if paid in full with cash) $31,800
   b. Down payment (if paid on contract)   —
   c. Transportation/Installation costs   1,000

2. Starting Inventory   25,000

3. Decorating and remodeling (fitting-up expense)   12,500

4. Deposits:
   a. Utilities, Telephone   500
   b. Rents   1,500
   c. Other (specify):   —

5. Fees:
   a. Professional (legal accounting)   3,800
   b. Licenses, permits, taxes   —
   c. Other (specify):   —

6. Advertising (initial)   5,000

7. Salaries/owner's draw until business opens   —

8. Other: —

                                        TOTAL STARTUP COSTS $81,100

E. Pro Forma Income Statements

NOTE: To arrive at Cost of Goods Sold, the following items were included—raw materials, factory labor and payroll taxes, and factory supplies.

PRO FORMA INCOME STATEMENTS

	Year 1		Year 2		Year 3	
Net Sales	$419,300	100.0	$798,800	100.0	$1,108,500	100.0
Cost of Goods Sold	279,200	66.6	532,600	66.7	823,800	74.3
Gross Margin	$140,100	33.4	$266,200	33.3	$284,700	25.7
Expenses						
Payroll expense	$ 54,500	13.0	$ 67,800	8.5	$ 82,300	7.4
Outside services	9,600	2.3	21,800	2.7	25,000	2.3
Business supplies	5,000	1.2	5,600	0.7	7,800	0.7
Repairs and maint.	1,400	0.3	4,800	0.6	4,000	0.4
Advertising	21,500	5.1	22,500	2.8	30,000	2.7
Car, delivery, travel	5,700	1.4	7,500	0.9	7,800	0.7
Acctg. & legal	5,600	1.3	7,200	0.9	7,700	0.7
Rent	18,000	4.3	18,000	2.3	18,000	1.6
Telephone	6,800	1.6	6,000	0.8	7,200	0.6
Utilities	3,600	0.9	4,800	0.6	5,600	0.5
Insurance	5,700	1.4	5,100	0.6	7,300	0.6
Taxes	1,000	0.2	1,000	0.1	2,000	0.2
Depreciation	8,200	2.0	15,800	2.0	17,400	1.6
Fees	3,000	0.7	1,800	0.2	4,000	0.4
Interest	20,800	5.0	20,300	2.5	19,800	1.8
Miscellaneous	7,300	1.7	9,000	1.1	10,000	0.9
Total Expenses	177,700	42.4	219,000	27.4	255,900	23.1
Profit (Loss) before tax	$(37,600)	(9.0)	$ 47,200	5.9	$ 28,800	2.6
Federal & state tax	—		1,600	0.2	4,800	0.4
Profit after tax	$(37,600)	(9.0)	$ 45,600	5.7	$ 24,000	2.2

F. Breakeven Analysis

First year: $\dfrac{\$177,700}{.334} = \$532,000$

Second year: $\dfrac{\$219,000}{.333} = \$658,000$

Third year: $\dfrac{\$255,900}{.257} = \$996,000$

YOUR
THREE-YEAR
BUSINESS
PLAN

YOUR THREE-YEAR BUSINESS PLAN.
This workbook is an integral part of *Raising Seed Money for Your Own Business.*

First Edition
Copyright © 1984 by Brian R. Smith

This book is manufactured in the United States of America. It is designed by Irving Perkins Associates and published by The Lewis Publishing Company, Fessenden Road, Brattleboro, Vermont 05301.

Distributed in the United States by E. P. Dutton, Inc., New York.

BUSINESS PLAN FOR

_____

(insert name of business)

Prepared by:
Date:

SUMMARY

(1. Give the name of the business, its location, and description of its physical facilities.)

(2. Briefly describe the product or service.)

(3. What market—consumer, industrial, government—are you serving? What segment of that market—teenagers, adult males—are you serving? What is unique about this business?)

(4. What are the overall goals of the business? Who are the people connected with the business?)

PURPOSE

The purpose of this prospectus is

TABLE OF CONTENTS

(Fill this in after the plan has been completed.
Be certain to show page numbers if the plan runs
to more than 15 pages.)

I. THE BUSINESS

A. *Business Description*

1. Name

2. Location

3. Physical Facilities

B. *Products or Services*

1. Description of Product Line

(Use more pages if necessary.)

2. Proprietary Considerations

C. *Management Plan*

1. Organizational Form and Structure

2. Resumés of Key People

3. Staffing Plan

4. Supporting Services

   Attorney:

   Accountant:

   Consultant:

   Insurance Agent:

   Advertising Agency:

D. *Operations Plan*

    1. Facilities and Equipment

2. Plans For Growth and Expansion

3. Overall Schedule

4. Process Description

E. *Risks*

1.

2.

3.

4.

5.

II. MARKETING PLAN

A. *Marketing Research*

    1. Description of the Market.

2. Industry Trends.

3. Target Market.

4. Competition.
   Competitor #1.

   Competitor #2.

   Competitor #3.

(Use more sheets if necessary.)

B. *Objectives and Strategy*

C. *Pricing Policy*

D. *Sales Terms*

E. *Method of Sales and Distribution*

F. *Customer Service*

G. *Advertising and Promotion*

H. *Forecasts*

III. FINANCIAL DATA

A. *Proposal*

(Center this on a single page.)

B. *Use of Proceeds*

Sources of Funds

1.

2.

3.

4.

Use of Proceeds

1.

2.

3.

4.

5.

6.

7.

8.

C. *Opening Day Balance Sheet*

Balance Sheet of _____
(name of business)

As of _____
(date business opens)

ASSETS	**LIABILITIES**
Cash $	Accounts Payable $
Inventory	Loans Payable

OWNER'S EQUITY

D. *Cash Flow Projections*

Startup Costs

1. Real estate, furniture, fixtures, machinery, equipment

    a. Purchase price (if paid in full with cash) $_____

    b. Down payment (if paid on contract)   _____

    c. Transportation/installation costs   _____

2. Starting inventory   _____

3. Decorating and remodeling   _____

4. Deposits

    a. Utilities, Telephone   _____

    b. Rents   _____

    c. Other (specify):   _____

5. Fees

    a. Professional (legal, accounting)   _____

    b. Licenses, permits, taxes   _____

    c. Other (specify):   _____

6. Advertising (initial)   _____

7. Salaries/owner's draw until business opens   _____

8. Other: _____

                                                    TOTAL STARTUP COSTS $_____

CASH FLOW PROJECTIONS (Second and Third Years)

Name of Business: _____   Address: _____   Prepared by: _____   Date: _____

		Year:						Year:				
		Qtr. 1	Qtr. 2	Qtr. 3	Qtr. 4	Year Totals		Qtr. 1	Qtr. 2	Qtr. 3	Qtr. 4	Year Totals	
4	Beginning cash												
5	Plus: Cash sales												
6	Collection of A/R												
7	Loans, other (specify)												
9	Total available cash												
10	Expenses												
11	Purchase of inventory												
12	Employee wages												
13	Payroll taxes & exp.												
14	Outside services												
15	Business suplies												
16	Repairs and maint.												
17	Advertising												
18	Car, delivery, travel												
19	Acctg. & legal												
20	Rent												
21	Telephone												
22	Utilities												
23	Insurance												
24	Taxes												
25	Equipment												
26	Other												
28	Loan repayment												
29	Miscellaneous												
30	Owner's withdrawal												
31	Total expenses												
32	Ending cash (9 less 31)												

24c

MONTHLY CASH FLOW PROJECTION

Name of Business: Address: Prepared by: Date:

			1	2	3	4	5	6	7	8	9	10	11	12	13 Total
	Year:														Total
		Month													12
															Months
1		Your investment														1
2	Less:	Startup costs														2
3																3
4		Beginning cash														4
5	Plus:	Cash sales														5
6		Collection of A/R														6
7		Loans, other (specify)														7
8																8
9	Total available cash															9
10	Expenses															10
11		Purchase of inventory														11
12		Employee wages														12
13		Payroll taxes & exp.														13
14		Outside services														14
15		Business suplies														15
16		Repairs and maint.														16
17		Advertising														17
18		Car, delivery, travel														18
19		Acctg. & legal														19
20		Rent														20
21		Telephone														21
22		Utilities														22
23		Insurance														23
24		Taxes														24
25		Equipment														25
26		Other														26
27																27
28		Loan repayment														28
29		Miscellaneous														29
30		Owner's withdrawal														30
31	Total expenses															31
32	Ending cash (9 less 31)															32
33																33
34																34
35																35

24b

MONTHLY CASH FLOW PROJECTION (Preliminary Worksheet)

Name of Business: Address: Prepared by: Date:

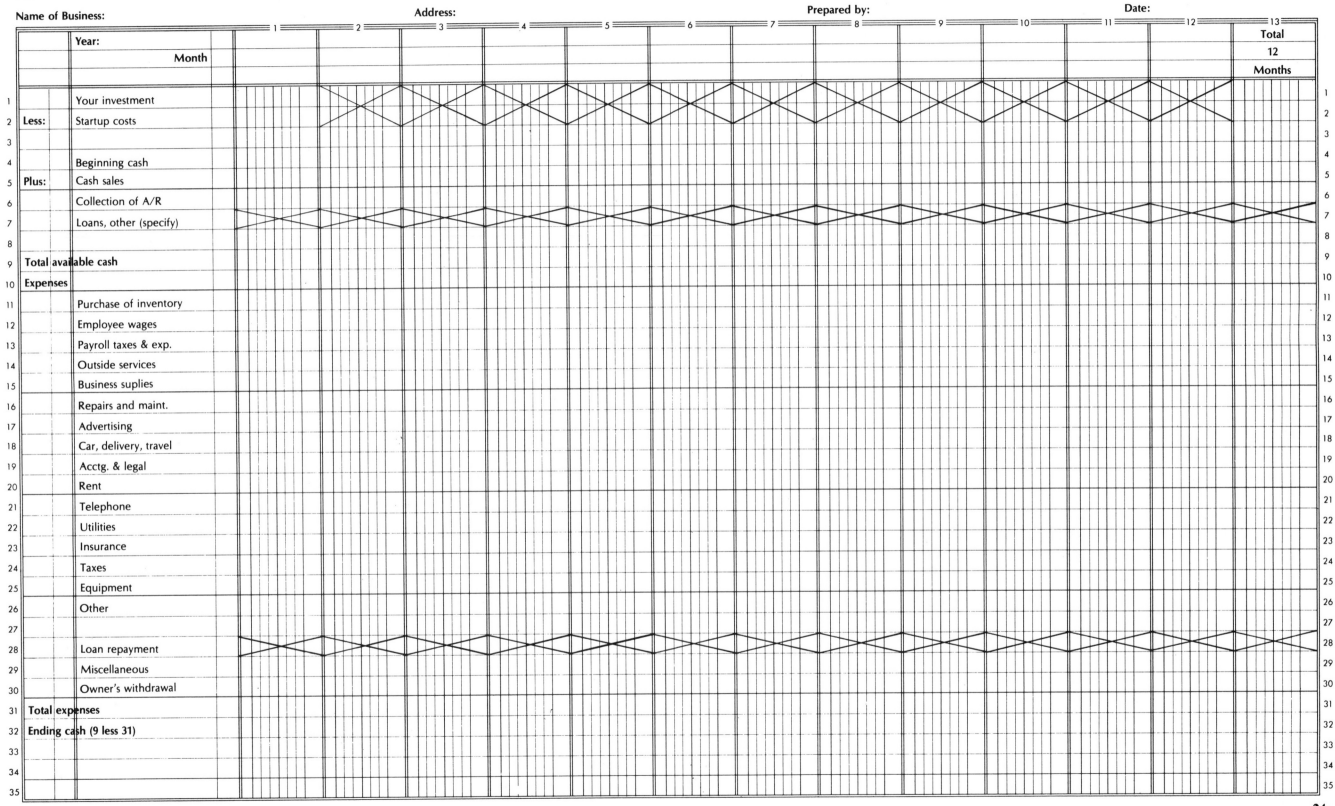

		Year: Month	1	2	3	4	5	6	7	8	9	10	11	12	Total 12 Months	
1		Your investment														1
2	Less:	Startup costs														2
3																3
4		Beginning cash														4
5	Plus:	Cash sales														5
6		Collection of A/R														6
7		Loans, other (specify)														7
8																8
9	Total available cash															9
10	Expenses															10
11		Purchase of inventory														11
12		Employee wages														12
13		Payroll taxes & exp.														13
14		Outside services														14
15		Business suplies														15
16		Repairs and maint.														16
17		Advertising														17
18		Car, delivery, travel														18
19		Acctg. & legal														19
20		Rent														20
21		Telephone														21
22		Utilities														22
23		Insurance														23
24		Taxes														24
25		Equipment														25
26		Other														26
27																27
28		Loan repayment														28
29		Miscellaneous														29
30		Owner's withdrawal														30
31	Total expenses															31
32	Ending cash (9 less 31)															32
33																33
34																34
35																35

24a

(Use the space below for any explanations about
the cash flow projections.)

E. *Pro Forma Income Statements*

(Use the space below for explanations, comments.)

PRO FORMA INCOME STATEMENT

Business_____

Period_____

                                                    _%_

Net Sales $

Cost of Goods Sold

Gross Margin $ _____ ___

Expenses

        Payroll expense $

        Outside services

        Business supplies

        Repairs and maintenance

        Advertising

        Car, delivery, travel

        Accounting and legal

        Rent

        Telephone and utilities

        Insurance

        Taxes

        Equipment rental

        Depreciation

        Postage and printing

        Interest

        Miscellaneous

        Other (specify):

Total Expenses   _____ ___

Profit (Loss) before tax $

Federal and State tax (%)   _____ ___

Profit after tax $

F. *Breakeven Analysis*

IV. APPENDICES